"Antony is internationally acclaimed for his work in the area of anxiety and is highly qualified to guide the reader along the path toward overcoming shyness. His ten simple solutions are sure to work for those willing to make the necessary commitment to self-change. His stepwise approach is explained with great clarity and simplicity. This is an essential guide for anyone seeking to overcome problems with shyness, social anxiety, and fear of public speaking. A timely and most important book."

—Jonathan R. T. Davidson, MD, director of the Anxiety and Traumatic Stress Program at the Duke University Medical Center

"Severe shyness and social anxiety are hidden epidemics, afflicting the lives of millions of people. Antony, a leading expert on shyness and social anxiety, has written a concise, easy-to-follow book that offers scientifically proven methods for overcoming these problems. This book is essential reading for anyone who wants to overcome shyness or social anxiety. It is also a valuable resource for anyone wanting a better understanding of the shy people in their lives."

—Steven Taylor, Ph.D., clinical psychologist and professor in the Department of Psychiatry at the University of British Columbia, Canada, and fellow of the Academy of Cognitive Therapy

D1167002

10 Simple Solutions to Shyness

How to Overcome Shyness, Social Anxiety & Fear of Public Speaking

MARTIN M. ANTONY, PH.D.

New Harbinger Publications, Inc.

Publisher's Note

Distributed in Canada by Raincoast Books

Copyright © 2004 by Martin M. Antony
        New Harbinger Publications, Inc.
        5674 Shattuck Avenue
        Oakland, CA 94609

Cover design by Amy Shoup
Cover image by Creatas
Text design by Michele Waters

ISBN-10 1-57224-348-1
ISBN-13 978-1-57224-348-4

Printed in the United States of America

New Harbinger Publications' website address: www.newharbinger.com

09   08   07

10   9   8   7   6

For my mentors, David H. Barlow and Richard P. Swinson

Contents

Acknowledgments

A big thank you to Kayla Sussell and Catharine Sutker at New Harbinger Publications for making the editorial process smooth and easy. Thanks also to Rebecca McEvilly for her careful assistance in proofreading and editing the manuscript, and to Dr. Mark Watling for his constructive comments on chapter 6. Finally, a special thank you to Cynthia Crawford for her never-ending support and encouragement.

Introduction

Almost everyone feels uncomfortable in social situations from time to time. In fact, feelings of social anxiety and shyness are perfectly normal. However, some people experience anxiety and shyness at a level that disturbs them, or that gets in the way of their day-to-day lives. If you worry excessively about what others think of you, or if you experience high levels of anxiety in situations such as parties, dating, public speaking, being observed, or meeting new people, this book is meant for you. Or, if you have a family member who is very anxious in social situations, this book will help you to better understand what your loved one is going through and what can be done to help.

This book differs from other books on shyness and social anxiety in a number of important ways. First, unlike some books, this one is based on the same types of treatment that have been proven by researchers to be effective for individuals who suffer from extreme social anxiety. The strategies described here are similar to those used by doctors and therapists who are experts in treating social anxiety.

Second, this book is briefer than almost all other books on the topic of overcoming shyness. It is meant for those who want an introduction to the strategies used to overcome social anxiety, but who prefer a briefer, more succinct format, rather than a larger, more detailed book. If you find the strategies described within to be useful, you may want to follow up this book with reading a more detailed workbook. For example, the *Shyness and Social Anxiety Workbook* (Antony and Swinson 2000) is filled with additional exercises, examples, and strategies. This and other recommended readings are listed at the end of this book.

Can a self-help book help a person to overcome his or her social anxiety? That's a difficult question to answer, because there has been very little research on the use of self-help treatments for shyness and social anxiety. However, there are at least a couple of reasons to think that a book like this may be useful. First, as mentioned above, well-controlled studies have demonstrated that the treatments described in this book are quite useful when administered by a therapist, in a clinical setting (see Antony and McCabe 2003). Second, there is research supporting the use of self-help treatments for other anxiety disorders, such as panic disorder (e.g., Gould and Clum 1995; Hecker et al. 1996).

At the very least, this book will provide you with information about effective strategies for overcoming shyness. If you find it difficult to use the techniques described here on your own, you will at least be a more informed consumer, and you'll be in a better position to seek out appropriate professional help.

Of course, simply *reading* this book will not be enough to begin to make important changes in your life. To get the most out of it, you'll need to practice the strategies over and over again, complete the various exercises thoroughly, and monitor your progress carefully. A journal or notebook will be the one essential tool you'll need to work through all the exercises in this book.

Many of the techniques described here require you to take notes, record your experiences, and monitor your use of various coping strategies. Exercises requiring the journal begin early on, so you may want to have it handy before you start reading chapter 1.

Reading a book about renovating your home won't make your house look any better, unless you follow up your reading with hard work. The same is true of reading about techniques for overcoming your social anxiety. Reducing your anxiety will involve making changes to the way you think and the way you behave in response to the specific situations that trigger your fear. Reading this book will not take long, but working through the strategies will be an ongoing process, lasting months, or even years. With a bit of patience and a lot of hard work, your efforts will pay off. Good luck!

1

Understanding Shyness and Social Anxiety

From the time she was a toddler, Sita has been quiet and withdrawn around people she doesn't know well. She often cannot think of what to say, and she worries that others may see her as boring or stupid. After starting a new job, it often takes her months to feel comfortable interacting with her coworkers. When she is with close friends and family, she is a completely different person: she is talkative, confident, and allows her sharp sense of humor to shine through.

Walter is quite comfortable interacting with others at parties and in other casual social situations. However, he is terrified of being the center of attention, particularly in work-related situations. Public speaking is nearly impossible for him. Even giving a brief report in a meeting with two or three other people present makes his heart pound. His fear of giving presentations and speaking in public restricted the types of courses he could take in college, as well as the directions his career has taken. For example, he's turned down several promotions for jobs that involve giving presentations.

Although he really wants to be in a relationship, José has not dated in several years. His friends tell him that he is attractive and interesting, yet he feels extremely uncomfortable when out on a date with a woman he doesn't know well. As he becomes more nervous, he begins to sweat profusely, loses his train of thought, and becomes very quiet. As a result, he often makes a poor first impression on his dates, confirming his worst fears that women find him unappealing.

Cindy does everything she can to avoid looking stupid in front of others. She constantly monitors how she comes across, and she rehearses her presentations for days to ensure they are memorized, and that she won't make a single mistake. If there is even a small chance that she will look foolish, she avoids the situation completely. For example, she avoids driving on busy streets for fear of making an error and having other drivers think, "Boy, that woman sure is an awful driver!"

Natasha is afraid of almost all social situations. Even asking for directions or inquiring about the time are nearly impossible for her. Walking down a busy street is torture, because she's convinced that others are watching her and thinking the worst. She always avoids parties, conversations with strangers, being the center of attention, and even talking on the phone—all for fear that she will make a bad impression on others. Recently, her isolation has led her to feeling very depressed. In fact, she sometimes feels as though she doesn't want to go on living unless things begin to change.

Lance just moved from the small town in Michigan where he grew up to Chicago, after being transferred for his job. Although he had lots of friends and an active social life in his hometown, he's finding it hard to meet new people in Chicago. He tends to be a little shy around new people, and he has been feeling a bit isolated. He's beginning to wonder whether he should have turned down his new job.

What these six very different people have in common is that they suffer from varying degrees of shyness and social anxiety. In Lance's case, his anxiety is centered primarily around meeting new people. Although it was never a problem in the past, his anxiety became more of an issue when he moved to a new city. At the other extreme, Natasha's social anxiety has left her almost housebound. In the other four examples, the anxiety is limited to particular social situations, such as dating and public speaking. Although each of these vignettes describes a different range of problems, every one of these individuals is excessively shy or socially anxious, and each of them is afraid of being judged negatively by others.

Shyness and Social Anxiety: Definitions

Shyness and social anxiety are related, but not identical concepts. The term *shyness* refers to a tendency to be withdrawn, anxious, or uncomfortable in situations involving interpersonal contact, such as conversations, dating, meeting new people, making small talk, talking on the phone, being assertive, dealing with conflict, or talking about oneself. Shyness is also associated with a tendency to be *introverted*; that is, shy individuals tend to be more inwardly focused and more socially withdrawn, compared to people who are more *extroverted*, or outgoing.

The term *social anxiety* refers to the experience of nervousness or discomfort in situations that may involve being observed, scrutinized, or judged by others. Certainly, shy people experience social anxiety when they must socialize with others, but there are times when people who are not particularly shy also may experience social anxiety.

For example, some people who are normally fairly outgoing may feel uncomfortable in situations where they are the center of attention, such as public speaking, eating in front of others, writing in front of others, using public bathrooms, performing in front of others, being observed, making a mistake in public, or working out in a public gym.

So, to summarize, if someone worries about being embarrassed or humiliated in a social or performance-related situation, that individual is said to be experiencing social anxiety. If the person is usually uncomfortable interacting with other people, he or she might be described as a shy person. Shy people, as well as people who are not particularly shy, may feel anxiety in social situations from time to time. Both shyness and social anxiety are normal experiences. In fact, almost everyone has these feelings from time to time. Distinguishing between normal anxiety and anxiety that may be a problem for you will be discussed later.

The Components of Social Anxiety

More often than not, social anxiety is experienced as an uncomfortable, and sometimes overwhelming, feeling that is difficult to describe or control. One strategy that can be useful for understanding your own feelings of shyness and social anxiety is to break them down into more manageable pieces. Most emotions, including anxiety, can be understood in terms of three components: a physical part (what you feel), a cognitive part (what you think), and a behavioral part (what you do).

THE PHYSICAL PART

When someone feels anxious in a social situation, a wide range of physical symptoms may be experienced. Often, the most disturbing symptoms are those that might be observed by others, such as sweating, shaking, blushing, and speaking unclearly. However, other symptoms of anxiety may include a racing or pounding heart, shortness of breath, nausea, dizziness, and other symptoms of physical arousal. When the person's fear is accompanied by at least four physical symptoms, it is sometimes referred to as a *panic attack*. The physical symptoms that take place during panic and fear are similar to those that occur during other intense emotions, sexual activity, physical exercise, and other experiences that trigger these types of symptoms.

THE COGNITIVE PART

The cognitive component of fear and anxiety refers to the types of thoughts, assumptions, beliefs, interpretations, and predictions that contribute to, and help to shape, the individual's feelings. In the case of anxiety, these beliefs usually focus on themes of danger or threat. Examples of beliefs that are often held by people who are socially anxious include the following:

- It is important that everybody like me, all of the time.

- If I give a presentation, I will make a fool of myself.

- If I make a mistake, people will think I am incompetent.

- I must always be interesting and entertaining.

- If someone stares at me, they must be thinking negative thoughts about me.

- If I am not liked by a particular person, no one will like me.

- It would be terrible to blush, shake, or sweat in front of others.

- People can see when I am anxious.

- I must try to hide my anxiety symptoms.

- Anxiety is a sign of weakness.

- I will not be able to speak if I am too anxious.

Not surprisingly, if you hold beliefs like these, you'll be prone to feeling anxious in social situations, particularly if you are exhibiting physical signs of anxiety. In many cases, beliefs like these are thought to trigger anxiety, or at least to keep the anxiety going once it has begun.

Researchers have demonstrated that in addition to having anxious thoughts, individuals with high levels of social anxiety tend to pay closer attention to information that confirms their beliefs than they do to information that contradicts their beliefs. For example, they may be more likely to notice the people in the audience who look critical or bored than those who seem attentive and interested.

Under certain circumstances, information may also be remembered particularly well if it is consistent with a person's anxious beliefs. For example, people who experience a lot of social anxiety are especially good at remembering faces that display negative expressions, compared to people who are less anxious in social situations (Lundh and Öst 1996). They are also more likely to report a history of childhood teasing than are people with other types of anxiety problems (McCabe et al. 2003). This may mean that people with social anxiety are teased more often in childhood. Or, it may mean that their *memories* of their experiences of being teased in childhood are stronger than are those of other people.

THE BEHAVIORAL PART

Avoidance is the most common behavioral feature of shyness and social anxiety. Often, people will avoid social situations completely, or at least escape from the feared situations after only a short time. However, people may also find more subtle ways to avoid situations or to protect themselves from social threat. They may wear extra makeup to hide blushing, avoid eye contact, ask other people questions to avoid talking about themselves, turn down the lights so people don't notice their anxiety symptoms, or have a couple of glasses of wine to help manage their anxiety.

Exercise: What Are the Components of Your Social Anxiety?

Try to break down your own social anxiety into its various parts. The next three times you feel anxious in a social situation, record the following information in your journal: (1) What situation triggered your anxiety? (2) What physical sensations did you experience? (3) What were your anxious thoughts, predictions, or beliefs? (4) What were your anxious behaviors?

When you write in your journal, be sure to write using the first person, so that your questions and answers refer only to yourself. As you work your way through this book, this will be true for all the exercises. Frame your questions this way:

1. What situation triggered my anxiety?

2. What physical sensations did I experience?

3. What were my anxious thoughts, predictions, or beliefs?

4. What were my anxious behaviors? In other words, what did I do to protect myself from anxiety? (For example, did I avoid or escape from the situation? Did I take other actions to reduce my fear?)

INTERACTIONS AMONG THE THREE COMPONENTS

The physical, cognitive, and behavioral components of anxiety interact with one another. The experience of anxiety can begin with a physical feeling (for example, shaky hands), which in turn triggers one or more anxious thoughts (for example, "if people notice my hands shaking, they will think I am a freak"), and various anxious behaviors (such as leaving a party fifteen minutes after arriving).

Or, the process can begin with a thought. For example, if you are thinking that your audience is unlikely to enjoy your presentation, that may trigger some physical responses, such as sweating or a racing heart. These arousal symptoms may trigger more intense anxious thoughts, and in the end, you may decide to avoid the situation.

The whole cycle also can begin with avoidance of a feared situation, or with some sort of protective behavior. Although these behaviors are effective for reducing feelings of anxiety in the short term, they often help to keep your anxiety alive over the long term by preventing you from ever learning that the situation is much more manageable than it feels. In fact, the more you avoid an unpleasant situation, the harder it is to enter that situation later. (Just ask yourself, "What is the hardest day of the week to drag yourself into work?" For many people, the answer is Monday.)

As mentioned in the introduction, you will find it essential to keep a journal as you work through the strategies described in this book. If you keep a journal, most of the exercises will be much easier to complete and keep organized.

Who Experiences Social Anxiety?

Almost everyone gets anxious in social situations from time to time. Comedian Jerry Seinfeld commented in one of his monologues that, "according to most studies, people's number one fear is public speaking. Number two fear is death. Death is number two! Now, this means, to the average person, if you have to go to a funeral, you're better off in the casket than doing the eulogy!" Seinfeld's conclusion is questionable, but it is clear that shyness and social anxiety are almost universal.

For example, in a series of surveys by psychologist Phillip Zimbardo and colleagues (e.g., Carducci and Zimbardo 1995; Henderson and Zimbardo 1999; Zimbardo, Pilkonis, and Norwood 1975), 40 percent of individuals described themselves as chronically shy, to the point of it being a problem. Of the remaining 60 percent, most people reported that they are shy in certain situations, or that they were shy previously. In fact, only 5 percent of people reported that they are never shy.

In research conducted at our Anxiety Treatment and Research Centre, we found that physical symptoms of social anxiety are common in the general population. In our study, most individuals reported physical symptoms of anxiety in social situations from time to time. Some of the most common of these include butterflies in the stomach, feelings of tension, blushing, trouble expressing oneself clearly, racing heart, stammering, a lump in the throat, sweating, shaking, and a tendency to smile, laugh, or talk uncontrollably or inappropriately (Purdon et al. 2001).

Are Shyness and Social Anxiety Always a Problem?

Most of the time, the only consequence of feeling socially anxious is the temporary discomfort that the individual experiences in the situation. In many cases, the anxiety is not noticeable to other people, and the symptoms don't interfere with the individual's functioning. If other people do notice the individual's anxiety, their response is usually not harsh. In fact, small amounts of shyness and social anxiety may be seen as positive attributes. Shyness may sometimes be seen as a sign of being modest or as one of the down-to-earth traits often viewed as refreshing and desirable.

In fact, not being socially anxious enough can be a problem for some individuals. We all know people who we wish were *more* concerned about what others think about them. For most of us, a little bit of shyness and social anxiety are useful traits to have. If you were *never* concerned about being judged by others, you would probably do things that would get you into trouble. You would always say exactly what's on your mind, without considering the effects on others. You would show up late for work, give presentations without preparing, and disclose information that is best kept private. Before long, others would begin to respond negatively, and there would be negative consequences. A certain amount of social anxiety protects you from doing things that could lead to severe social consequences.

WHEN ARE SHYNESS AND SOCIAL ANXIETY PROBLEMS?

Social anxiety becomes a problem when it happens too frequently and too intensely, so much so that the person is distressed by the level of the anxiety, has difficulty functioning, and is unable to achieve important life goals. For example, a salesman who becomes anxious and shuts down whenever he has to converse with potential customers probably will find that his anxiety interferes with his ability to make a good income. Similarly, a woman who wants to be in a relationship but turns down every opportunity to date, for fear of making a bad impression, is likely to feel discouraged and stuck as a result of her anxiety. In these cases, social anxiety is clearly a problem.

When social anxiety becomes a significant problem, mental health professionals often refer to the condition as *social phobia* or *social anxiety disorder*. This is an extreme form of social anxiety that causes considerable distress or impairment in day-to-day functioning. Social phobia can have a severe impact on many different domains of living, including close relationships, education, career, social life, hobbies, and other areas of functioning.

There has been some disagreement across several studies as to how prevalent social phobia is, but our best estimate, based on a study by Canadian researchers, puts it in the probable range of 7 percent of the total population (Stein, Walker, and Forde 1994). In other words, almost one in fifteen individuals suffers from social phobia, and many more have milder manifestations of social anxiety that can be a problem from time to time. Social anxiety occurs frequently in both men and women, and across cultures, although different people may show their anxiety in different ways.

Exercise: How Shyness Interferes with Your Life

Pick up your journal and on a fresh page entitled "How Shyness Interferes with My Life," write down the ways in which your shyness or social anxiety interferes with your life. How would things be different if shyness or performance anxiety were not a problem for you? Would you have more friends? Different friends? A different job? Different hobbies? How differently would you spend your time? Would your relationships with others change?

Causes of Social Anxiety

Nobody knows exactly what causes people to become socially anxious, although we do understand some of the factors that most likely play a role. The underlying causes of shyness and performance anxiety are complex, and probably differ somewhat from person to person.

Like other forms of anxiety, social anxiety probably developed through evolution as a way to protect us from potential dangers or threats. As mentioned earlier, our social anxiety helps us to keep our impulses in check, so we don't continually do or say things that we will regret later. Still, for some individuals, the anxiety is excessive, unrealistic, and often not particularly helpful. In other words, they have too much of a good thing.

For several decades, researchers have been trying to understand the factors that cause some of us to develop significant problems with social anxiety. Some of the factors they've uncovered include the following.

GENETICS. Social anxiety tends to run in families. Statistically, a person who has a parent or sibling with social phobia is about ten times more likely to develop social phobia than is someone whose family members don't have social phobia (Stein et al. 1998). In addition, there is some evidence that genetics (rather than exclusively environmental factors, e.g., learning) may partly explain the transmission of social anxiety from one generation to the next. Traits often associated with social anxiety (e.g., introversion) tend to be quite heritable.

THE BRAIN. Recent studies have shown that when an individual experiences anxiety related to a social or performance situation, certain areas of the brain are more active than others (Tillfors et al. 2001; Tillfors et al. 2002), as indicated by differences in blood flow across different brain regions. Furthermore, treatment for social phobia (with either medication or psychological treatment) appears to lead to changes in these patterns of brain activity (Furmark et al. 2002). Although research findings are mixed, *neurotransmitters* (the chemical messengers that transmit information from one brain cell to another), such as serotonin and dopamine, probably play a role in social anxiety as well.

LEARNING. It is well established that learning and experience can play an important role in the development of fear. In some cases, negative life experiences (such as being teased or criticized in childhood) may contribute to higher levels of social anxiety. Growing up with other people who are shy or socially anxious also may play a role, because we often learn how to behave by watching others, including our parents. Finally, being told repeatedly how important it is to always make a good impression on others may lead some people to become overly concerned about making mistakes and about being judged negatively.

ANXIOUS BELIEFS. As discussed earlier, a person's beliefs also seem to contribute to the tendency to feel anxious in social situations. If social situations are mistakenly viewed as dangerous or threatening, the person holding such a view is far likelier to feel uncomfortable and vulnerable when exposed to these situations. People who are socially anxious often believe (1) that it is extremely important to make a positive impression on others, (2) they are very likely to make a negative impression on others, and (3) that the result of that negative impression will be a disaster. No wonder social anxiety can be such a chronic problem for some people.

ANXIOUS BEHAVIORS. As discussed earlier in this chapter, anxious behaviors like avoidance can help to maintain shyness and feelings of anxiety over the long term. The more you try to protect yourself from feeling anxious, or from making a bad impression, the more likely you are to continue feeling anxious down the road. Overcoming shyness will involve confronting the situations that make you feel uncomfortable.

Exercise: What Are the Factors Contributing to Your Social Anxiety?

Are you aware of any factors that may have contributed to your social anxiety problems? If so, record them on a fresh page in your journal. To help you get started, answer these questions: Were you always anxious in social or performance situations? Did you have any negative experiences related to social situations? Are your parents or other family members very shy? Might you have learned some of these behaviors from them?

Effective Treatments for Social Anxiety: An Overview

There are many different approaches to coping with feelings of anxiety. This book discusses strategies that have been shown to be particularly useful, based on carefully controlled studies. These treatments generally fall under two main categories: cognitive behavioral therapy (CBT) and medications. Chapter 6 reviews medication treatments that can help with social anxiety. Chapters 3, 4, and 5 review cognitive and behavioral techniques for dealing with social anxiety. These include *cognitive strategies* for learning to change your anxious beliefs, *exposure-based techniques* for learning to directly confront anxiety-provoking social situations, and *communication training* for learning to communicate more effectively. Together, these CBT strategies provide proven methods for learning how to cope more effectively with your feelings of shyness and anxiety in social situations.

2

Plan for Change

Chapter 1 reviewed the nature of shyness and social anxiety, as well as providing you with an overview of available treatments. Now, the purpose of this chapter is to help you decide whether you are ready to start working to overcome your social anxiety, and to consider what types of changes to make.

Is This the Best Time to Make Changes?

As stated in chapter 1, social anxiety and shyness are not necessarily a problem. Most people experience excessive social anxiety from time to time, and they get by just fine. Even when social anxiety is a problem, it is not necessarily the case that an individual should put everything aside to focus on overcoming his or her anxiety right away. In fact, you may have other demands or priorities that at any given time might interfere with working on your social anxiety.

Although there is never a perfect time to embark on the path to change, your chances of getting the most out of this book are likely to be higher if you answer yes to the following questions. Circle the appropriate answer.

- Do I want to become less shy or socially anxious? Would my quality of life improve if I were to become more comfortable in social situations? Is this something that matters to me?
  Yes   No

- Am I willing to feel uncomfortable in the short term in order to become more comfortable in social and performance situations later? (Note that overcoming anxiety usually involves confronting feared situations. See chapter 4.)
  Yes   No

- Am I able to put significant amounts of time (e.g., five to ten hours per week) into working on my social anxiety over the next few months?
  Yes   No

- If I am having other difficulties (such as family problems, stress at work, etc.), will I able to put these problems aside, at least to some extent, so I can focus on changing my social anxiety?
  Yes   No

Another question to consider is whether your social anxiety is a result of another problem. For example, if you have an eating disorder, and you are very worried about others passing negative judgments about your weight or eating habits, you may find it challenging to work on your social anxiety without also working on your problematic eating behaviors and body image. If your social anxiety is related to having others observe the symptoms of another problem, such as an eating disorder, depression, substance abuse, or even a medical condition, the strategies in this book may still be useful. Nevertheless, it may also be important for you to find ways to manage the other problem contributing to your social anxiety and shyness.

The Costs and Benefits of Changing

Making the decision to work on your social anxiety comes with both costs and benefits. The benefits may include greater self-confidence, increased ease in social situations, more enjoyment of life, improved relationships, new opportunities (such as making new friends, taking advantage of new job prospects), and mastery of some learning strategies that can be applied to other emotional problems, such as irritability or depressed mood.

Typical costs include such matters as the time commitment needed to read the text and do the exercises, having to take actions that will increase your anxiety in the short term, mild side effects (if you choose to take medications; see chapter 6), and financial expenses, for example, the money you will spend to go out more often, or the cost of medications or treatment with a professional therapist should you decide to see one. The decision that you must make is whether the benefits of becoming less shy outweigh the potential costs. If they do, then trying to reduce your social anxiety may well be worth it.

Exercise: What Are the Costs and Benefits of Changing?

Now, on a fresh page in your journal, record the benefits and costs that will arise while you work to overcome your difficulties with shyness and social anxiety. These may include some of the examples listed above, but they also may include costs and benefits that are unique to you and your situation.

Deciding What to Work On

In all likelihood, there are a number of different social and performance situations that trigger your anxiety. The first important step to take in preparing to overcome your anxiety is to identify what you would like to change, and in what order. Some questions to ask yourself include the following:

WHAT ARE THE SITUATIONS THAT TRIGGER MY ANXIETY? Examples may include meeting new people, engaging in small talk, starting conversations, keeping conversations going, dating, family gatherings, talking on the phone, talking about myself, having lunch with coworkers, being the center of attention, making mistakes in front of others, writing in front of others, using public bathrooms, eating or drinking in front of others, public speaking, participating in meetings, working out in front of others, and being observed by others.

WHICH OF THESE SITUATIONS IS THE MOST IMPORTANT TO ME? In which situations does my anxiety interfere most with how I want live my life?

FOR WHICH OF THESE SITUATIONS IS MY ANXIETY GOING TO BE THE EASIEST TO CHANGE? What are the obstacles to overcoming my anxiety in relation to these various situations?

Exercise: Rate the Situations That Are Uncomfortable for You

In your journal, make a list of social and performance situations that you find difficult and uncomfortable. Then, beside each item, record a rating to reflect how important it is for you to feel comfortable in that situation. Use a scale ranging from 0 to 100, where 0 = not at all important, and 100 = extremely important.

As you work through the material in this book, the idea will be to start by working on the situations that are most important to you. There is no point spending a lot of time learning to be comfortable in situations that you don't really care about. Usually, people begin by working on situations that are somewhat challenging, but not too difficult. If you begin by working on more manageable situations, you will be more likely to experience some success early in the process, which will give you the courage to tackle some of the more challenging situations later on.

SETTING GOALS

Setting goals is an essential part of overcoming your difficulties with shyness and social anxiety. Identifying your goals will help to keep you on track as you work to achieve them. Goal setting also makes it possible to evaluate whether you are in fact making the changes that you set out to make. As you set goals, try to make them as specific as possible. The more detailed your goal, the easier it will be to understand what needs to be done to meet it, and to measure whether you have achieved it. Here are two examples of general goals that are too vague to be helpful, each followed by a more detailed specific goal, described in a way that is more likely to be useful.

General goal: to be more comfortable in groups.

Specific goal: to feel comfortable making small talk at office parties, while making eye contact, and while speaking loudly enough that others can hear me easily.

General goal: to experience only mild anxiety while speaking in public.

Specific goal: to experience only mild anxiety while presenting a report at a meeting with four or five of my coworkers present, on a topic that I know well.

It is also useful to define goals for the short term, the long term, and for various other periods in between. Short-term goals are objectives or aims for the near future (for example, today, tomorrow, or next week). Medium-range goals could reflect accomplishments you would like to achieve over the next few months. Long-term goals might be those that you would like to achieve over a period of a few years. Examples of short-term, medium-range, and long-term goals for someone who experiences anxiety around dating are provided below:

Short-term goal: to approach Jennifer on Monday about attending my brother's wedding with me next month.

Medium-range goal: to increase the frequency of my dating to about once a week over the next four months.

Long-term goal: to be in a steady relationship in two years.

You can actually set goals for any time period that makes sense to you. In some cases, you can set even shorter-term goals (for example, what you want to achieve in the next few hours), or very long-term goals (for example, where you want to be in your career in twenty years).

Exercise: Make of List of Your Goals

In your journal, make a list of goals for overcoming your difficulties with shyness and social anxiety. Try to come up with ten to twenty goals, categorized as short-term, medium-range, and long-term objectives. Remember to be as specific as possible about what you would like to achieve, and your timeline for achieving it.

Keep Your Expectations Realistic

It has probably taken years for you to get to where you are today, so it wouldn't be reasonable to assume that everything will change overnight as a result of reading this book. While it's true that some people who use the strategies described within do make dramatic transformations in their social anxiety, for most people, the changes happen gradually. Furthermore, from time to time, people who have had success changing their social anxiety still may continue struggling with social anxiety, although typically at a much lower level.

If you use the techniques described in these chapters, the chances are good that you will enjoy a significant reduction in your shyness and anxiety. However, don't be surprised if you continue to experience anxiety in certain situations, or at certain times. In fact, you may always be a bit on the shy side, compared to others. The goal of this book is not to eliminate all anxiety, but rather to bring your anxiety down to a level at which it interferes much less with your day-to-day life, and to help you to reach a point at which you are less concerned about your performance.

3

Change the Way You Think

Imagine for a moment that you were convinced (1) that there was very little chance that you would ever make a negative impression on others, and (2) that the consequences of making a negative impression were minimal—in other words, that most of the time it doesn't matter what people think of you. What effect would that have on your shyness and social anxiety?

Scientists who study shyness have generally found that people's beliefs, interpretations, assumptions, predictions, and memory processes play an important role in whether they tend to experience excessive anxiety in social and performance situations. Specifically, researchers have discovered that, on average, compared to people who are low in social anxiety, people who are very shy or socially anxious:

- Are more critical of their own performance, such as during a conversation or while giving a speech (Rapee and Lim 1992; Stopa and Clark 1993).

- Rate their own performance more negatively than do independent observers. In other words, if you are particularly shy, chances are that other people are not nearly as critical of your behavior as you are. In contrast, for people low in social anxiety, self-ratings and observer ratings tend to be quite close together (Norton and Hope 2001).

- Assume that negative social events are more probable and more likely to have extreme negative consequences. This tendency tends to decrease following treatment for social anxiety (Foa et al. 1996).

- Spend more time (when reading lists of words) looking at words that they find threatening, such as "presentation," compared to more neutral words, such as "house" (Holle, Neely, and Heimberg 1997). These findings have been viewed by researchers as evidence that social anxiety is associated with a tendency to focus excessively on information that indicates possible "danger" in social situations.

- Interpret ambiguous facial expressions (such as a "flat" look on someone's face) as negative (Winton, Clark, and Edelmann 1995). Shy individuals are also better able to remember photos of faces they have seen previously, particularly faces with negative expressions (Lundh and Öst 1996).

- Compare themselves to others who they believe are much better than they are, which typically leads to increased levels of anxiety and depression. In contrast, people low in social anxiety are more likely to compare themselves to others whom they perceive as similar to or worse off than they are, and they tend not to feel as bad after making social comparisons (Antony et al. in press).

- Overestimate the extent to which their physical symptoms of anxiety (e.g., blushing) are visible to others (Mulkens et al. 1999), and they tend to overestimate the degree to which others negatively evaluate them based on whether they exhibit physical symptoms of anxiety (Roth, Antony, and Swinson 2001).

Taken together, these studies clearly demonstrate that shyness is associated with a negative thinking style—and that this pattern probably helps to maintain a person's social anxiety over time.

Cognitive Therapy

In the 1960s, long before there was any systematic research on the role played by anxious thinking in the development and maintenance of anxiety, several influential psychologists and psychiatrists began to observe in their clients and patients a strong relationship between negative thinking and negative emotions, such as anxiety and depression. The best known of these individuals is probably psychiatrist Aaron T. Beck, although psychologists Albert Ellis and Donald Meichenbaum also made important contributions in this area. Each of these pioneers developed their own therapies specifically designed to change negative thinking, and thereby decrease the impact of negative moods. These treatments share many features, although there are also subtle differences among them.

Beck's form of treatment, called *cognitive therapy* (the word *cognition* refers to thinking) has been particularly influential in the area of anxiety disorders, and much of the information from this chapter is derived from his work (Beck, Emery, and Greenberg 1985). In addition, several of the strategies described in this chapter can be credited to a second generation of cognitive therapy pioneers who applied Beck's work to the treatment of social phobia, shyness, and related problems. Some of the other individuals who have influenced the material in this chapter include psychologists Richard Heimberg (e.g., Heimberg and Becker 2002), Ron Rapee (e.g., Rapee and Sanderson 1998), and psychiatrist David Burns (1999).

The underlying assumption of cognitive therapy is that people's anxiety, depression, and other negative moods are directly influenced by the ways in which they interpret events and situations. Basically, if you interpret a situation as safe, you will feel comfortable and content. However, if you view a situation as threatening or dangerous, you are more likely to feel anxious, frightened, and uncomfortable.

Although our appraisals regarding the level of threat in a situation are sometimes realistic, often they are not. Sometimes people underestimate the degree of danger (for example, when driving intoxicated), and other times, people overestimate the degree of danger (for example, avoiding flying, even though only one in ten million commercial flights actually ends in a crash). Cognitive therapy assumes that it is not situations, per se, that trigger anxiety. Rather, it is our interpretations of these situations that make us anxious.

Cognitive therapy has a number of goals:

- To help individuals to become more aware of the beliefs, predictions, and assumptions that influence their negative emotions.

- To encourage people to view their beliefs as guesses or hypotheses about the way things may be, rather than as definite facts.

- To replace unrealistic assumptions and beliefs with more realistic ways of thinking by keeping the big picture in mind, considering all of the evidence for and against a particular belief, and conducting small experiments to test out whether the negative beliefs are true.

Identifying Your Anxious Thoughts

Before you can begin to change your anxious thoughts, it is important to be able to recognize them, ideally when they are occurring. For some people, recognizing their anxious thoughts is easy. For others, it's more difficult. Anxious beliefs may be so entrenched, habitual, and automatic that they take place outside of conscious awareness. If this is so for you, you may experience a feeling of dread or discomfort in social situations, and not really know what it is you're afraid of. With practice, it will likely become easier to identify your thoughts. However, if you continue to have difficulty labeling your anxious thoughts, don't despair. Even if you are never able to identify your specific anxious thoughts, you may still benefit from using some of the other strategies described in this book.

There are several different ways in which cognitive therapists classify types of negative thinking. First, they often discuss different *levels* of negative thinking, ranging from thoughts that occur relatively quickly, triggered by particular situations, to more deeply held assumptions that influence how a person views the world. A second way in which negative thinking styles are classified is with respect to the specific type of cognitive error that is being made. Each of these ways of discussing negative thinking can be useful, and both are reviewed below.

Levels of Negative Thinking

Cognitive therapists often describe three levels of negative thinking: negative automatic thoughts, intermediate beliefs, and core beliefs. Any or all of these can contribute to feelings of shyness and social anxiety.

Negative automatic thoughts are beliefs that are usually triggered in specific situations. They can occur very quickly, may be outside of your awareness, and usually lead to some sort of emotional or behavioral response. In the case of social anxiety, the emotional response may be fear or anxiety, and the behavioral response often involves trying to escape from the situation or trying to engage in some other behavior to decrease the discomfort and to protect oneself from feeling threatened. Often, negative automatic thoughts are not based in reality. Instead, they are biased in a negative direction. Examples of negative automatic thoughts include:

- Nobody at this party wants to talk to me.

- My presentation is not going well.

- People will notice my hands are shaking.

- I'm making a fool of myself.

- I will never get the job I just interviewed for.

- People find me very boring.

Intermediate beliefs take place at a deeper level than negative automatic thoughts. In fact, intermediate beliefs can give rise to negative automatic thoughts under the right circumstances. Intermediate beliefs are rules that people have regarding the way things are or about the way things should be. Sometimes they can be phrased in terms of an "if-then" statement. Examples of intermediate beliefs include:

- If people notice my sweating, then they will think there is something seriously wrong with me.

- If I make a mistake, then people will think I'm an idiot.

- It is important for everyone to like me.

- It is essential that I hide my feelings of anxiety from others.

- It is important to always do a good job.

Core beliefs represent the deepest level of thinking. These are the most basic assumptions that people hold about themselves and the world. Core beliefs are often held very strongly and can have a profound effect on how we interpret events. These beliefs often are the most difficult to change; it is almost as if they are part of our basic personality. Examples of core beliefs include:

- People cannot be trusted.
- I am an unlovable person.

HOW FAULTY THINKING CREATES ANXIETY

This section reviews a number of specific ways in which people often misinterpret, misperceive, and miscalculate in the midst of social and performance situations. The more an individual engages in these types of thinking, the more fear and anxiety he or she is likely to experience. Keep in mind that these are not really discrete types of thinking, in that a particular thought may fit into more than one category. For example, the thought "my boss will think I'm incompetent" may be an example of both probability overestimation and mind reading.

Also, remember that making these types of "thinking errors" doesn't mean you are stupid or that you don't know how to think! Everyone makes errors in judgment and engages in distorted thinking from time to time. There is no relationship between intelligence and anxiety. Furthermore, engaging in distorted thinking is not a problem in and of itself. In the case of excessive social anxiety, one's thinking is biased in such a way that it increases anxiety and discomfort in social situations, which in turn leads to impairment in relationships or in other areas of one's life. It is the consequences of distorted thinking that is the problem.

ASSUMING THE WORST WILL OCCUR

Probability overestimations involve exaggerated beliefs about the chances of something bad happening, or predictions that something negative is likely to happen even though, in reality, it is unlikely to occur. Examples of probability overestimation include the following:

- Believing that you can never find a job, even though there is a reasonably good chance that you will find a job if you send out résumés or job applications.

- Being convinced that you will make a complete fool of yourself during a presentation, despite the fact that most people in the audience think your presentation is fine.

- Being sure that others at a party are unlikely to find you interesting, even though people who know you enjoy your company.

- Assuming that others are certain to notice your shaky hands, even though most people are not even aware of your hands.

CATASTROPHIC THINKING

Catastrophic thinking (also called "catastrophizing") involves exaggerating the importance of a particular event or outcome. Typically, this involves predicting that a particular outcome would be completely unmanageable, overwhelming, and awful—although, in reality, the feared consequences would be manageable if they were to occur. Examples of catastrophic thoughts include:

- It would be terrible if I were to blush in front of someone else.

- I don't think I could handle it if someone were to notice my sweating.

- It would be completely embarrassing if I were to stumble on my words during my talk.

- I can't handle having someone else be upset with me.

ALL-OR-NOTHING THINKING

All-or-nothing thinking is the tendency to see things in black and white, without being able to consider the grays. This type of thinking involves an oversimplification of situations and a bias to view one's performance as either right or wrong (or, good versus bad). When people engage in all-or-nothing thinking, they fail to see the complexities in situations and the exceptions to their rules about how things should be. Perfectionism is often association with all-or-nothing thinking, a topic that is discussed in chapter 10. Examples of all-or-nothing thinking include:

- If even one person doesn't like me, I feel like I'm a complete failure.

- It is essential that I always make a perfect impression on everyone I meet.

- I should be able to control all of my anxiety symptoms at all times.

MIND READING

Mind reading involves making assumptions about what other people are thinking in the absence of any hard evidence. This particular cognitive error is a big one for people who are quite shy or socially anxious. In fact, the very definition of social anxiety requires that a person be concerned about being judged negatively by others. Assuming that others are thinking bad thoughts about you is essentially a form of mind reading. Some examples of thoughts that could be considered to be mind reading include:

- My date finds me unattractive.

- People find me boring.

- If my boss notices my hands shaking, she will think I am too nervous to do my job.

PERSONALIZATION

Personalization involves blaming yourself (and only yourself) for negative outcomes in social situations, even though the situations are complex and many factors have likely contributed to the outcomes. Here are some examples:

- Assuming that if your spouse is upset with you, that's proof that there's something wrong with who you are. It is equally possible that your spouse is engaging in distorted thinking and is overreacting to the situation. Or, perhaps the conflict has arisen because of both something you did and your spouse's overreaction.

- Assuming that a sleepy audience is a sign that you are not a good presenter, when in reality there are many factors that determine an audience's level of interest—the topic, the time of day, the length of the presentation, the presenter's style, and how relevant the material is to the audience's needs.

- Assuming that a fizzling conversation is your fault, whereas both parties are equally responsible for keeping a conversation going. Of course, this is not to say that it really matters whether a conversation fizzles; eventually all conversations come to an end.

SELECTIVE ATTENTION AND MEMORY

Selective attention and memory refer to one's tendency to focus only on information that is consistent with one's beliefs.

In social anxiety, this involves paying extra close attention to signals that one is being judged negatively. Examples of this style of thinking include:

- Feeling bad after your annual performance review at work because you are focusing on the one or two areas for improvement and ignoring all the positive comments in the report.

- Noticing the people in the audience who seem bored or restless during your talk, and ignoring the people who appear to be enjoying the presentation.

- Remembering in detail the times when you were teased about the way you looked or the way you behaved, but not paying much attention to the positive feedback or compliments that you've received over the years.

Figuring Out What You Are Thinking

For many people, one of the hardest steps in the process of changing anxious thoughts is figuring out which anxious thoughts are being experienced in the first place. As reviewed earlier, thoughts, assumptions, and predictions often occur so quickly that we are not aware of them. If you are having difficulty identifying your own anxious thoughts, here are some strategies that you may find useful.

- Pay attention to your shifts in anxiety, no matter how small. When you notice an increase or decrease in the anxiety you feel, that is the time to ask yourself, "What am I thinking right now?" and "How have my thoughts changed, compared to a few minutes ago?"

- Remember, most anxious thoughts can be phrased in the form of a prediction. Ask yourself,

"What do I think is going to happen?" or "What might this person (or these people) be thinking about me?"

- Sometimes, anxious thoughts are very general (such as the belief that someone won't like you). Other times, they may be more specific, focused on a belief that someone won't like a particular aspect of who you are or what you do. To identify more specific predictions, try asking yourself, "Am I afraid that others will view me as incompetent? Stupid? Ugly? Boring? Nerdy? Less valuable? Weak? Crazy? Overly anxious?"

- If you are afraid of others noticing your anxiety symptoms, try to identify which symptoms you think they are most likely to notice. Shaking? Sweating? Blushing? Shaky voice? Strained facial expression? Losing your train of thought?

- Often, the reason people feel anxious about being judged by others is that they believe negative judgments by others either can lead to significant negative consequences, or can be a sign that there is indeed something wrong with them. In other words, if you are feeling anxiety in social situations, you may believe that you deserve to be judged by others, and that the flaws that others supposedly see in you are real. To identify this type of thinking, it is helpful to ask yourself questions such as these: "What if my date doesn't want to go out with me again? What terrible things will that mean about me?" or "What do I think will happen if the audience finds my presentation to be overly simple?"

Exercise: Identify and Record Your Anxious Thoughts

It is useful to keep a record of your anxious thoughts as they occur. For the next few weeks (or for as long as you are working through the strategies in this book), try to identify and record your anxious thoughts in your journal. If it is inconvenient to write down your thoughts while in the situation (for example, in the middle of your presentation or while eating dinner with friends), try recording your fearful predictions and beliefs either just before entering the situation or immediately after leaving the situation.

Strategies for Changing Your Anxious Thoughts

In order to reduce your shyness and social anxiety to a more manageable level, it is important to change the way you think about your interactions with other people and to learn to be less concerned about how you come across to others. This is not to say that it isn't at all important what others think of you. To be sure, we all pass judgment on one another from time to time, and, in some circumstances, making a bad impression on others can lead to serious negative consequences.

Still, in most cases, we cannot control the impressions we make on others, and we usually are unaware of what others are thinking. Our assumptions about what other people notice and about what they find attractive or unattractive are often completely wrong. Also, the consequences of making a bad impression are fortunately much less significant than we think, most of the time.

The goal of this chapter is to help you to stop assuming that your anxious beliefs are true, and to begin to view situations from a wider perspective—considering not just your own interpretations and beliefs, but also other possible ways to view social and performance situations. Remember, it is not the feared situations that trigger your anxiety, but rather your interpretations of those situations. In the following sections, specific methods are described to be used to challenge your anxious thoughts and to replace them with more balanced or realistic ways of thinking about the situations that make you uncomfortable.

CONSIDER ALTERNATIVE BELIEFS AND EXAMINE THE EVIDENCE

Rather than treating your anxious beliefs as hard facts, it is much more helpful to view them as guesses about they way things are, and to examine all the evidence that supports and refutes your beliefs. When you have an anxious thought, some useful questions to ask yourself include:

- What are the facts?

- Are there some facts that support my anxious thought?

- Are there some facts that don't support my anxious thought?

- Are the facts supporting my anxious thought ironclad or could they also support another thought?

- What's the big picture?

- Are there other ways of viewing this situation?

- Do I know for sure that my prediction will come true?

- What does my past experience tell me about the likelihood of my thoughts coming true?

- Are there times when I have experienced anxious thoughts that didn't come true?

- Are there facts or statistics that can help me to decide whether my prediction is likely to come true?

By considering alternative explanations and interpretations, and allowing yourself to examine all the evidence, you may find that your original belief is not as "true" as it seemed to be, and that realization should help to reduce your anxiety. Here are some examples of how examining the evidence can help to reduce anxiety.

Imagine you are walking down the street, and you see a coworker whom you don't know particularly well. You say hello and the other person doesn't respond. How would you feel? For some people who are very anxious about being negatively judged, the feelings triggered by such an event may include anxiety, sadness, or anger, especially if they believe that the other person ignored them. Experiencing negative thoughts such as, "That person can't even bother to remember who I am" or, "I guess that person doesn't like me" might be upsetting to someone who is prone to shyness and social anxiety.

But are these the only possible interpretations for this situation? In reality, there are many different reasons why a coworker might not say hello to you in this hypothetical situation. Perhaps the coworker was distracted or didn't hear you say hello. Or maybe the coworker did say hello, and you didn't hear him or her. Perhaps the coworker wasn't feeling well. Maybe he or she was feeling too ill, depressed, upset, or hungry to say hello. Perhaps the coworker was in a hurry to get somewhere, or perhaps that person is very shy. Maybe the coworker just isn't the type who likes stopping to say hello to people on the street. Or, perhaps the person didn't recognize you outside of the context of your normal workplace.

In other words, there are lots of reasons that have nothing to do with you that could explain why that person didn't say hello. After examining the alternative explanations, often it becomes easy to see that the original anxious explanation is much less likely to be true.

But what if it is true? What if the coworker doesn't remember who you are, or what if (heaven forbid!) the coworker doesn't like you? Should that be devastating? What does it mean if someone doesn't like you? Should everyone like you? Well, to answer that question, let's look at the belief "It is important for everyone to like me." This belief is commonly held by people who experience excessive social anxiety.

Is it really important that everyone like you? Well, it is probably important that some people like you, for example, your boss and your spouse. But what if a coworker who doesn't know you well doesn't like you? What would that mean about you? Would it mean that there is something wrong with you? Asking some key questions can help you to examine the relevant evidence in order to come to a realistic conclusion.

Key Questions to Ask Yourself

First, can you think of anyone who is liked by everyone? Perhaps a celebrity, like an actor or politician? No matter how hard you try, you probably won't be able to think of anyone who is liked by all people. According to some biographers (e.g., Dils 2003; Sebba 1998), even Mother Teresa had her critics! If Mother Teresa wasn't liked by everyone, how likely is it that you or I will be liked by everyone?

Is it even possible to be liked by everyone? Is it possible for each and every person out there to find you interesting and attractive? Again, the answer is probably not. The very qualities that make an individual interesting, likable, and attractive to one person are the same features that make that individual less attractive or likable to someone else. If this wasn't true, we would all vote for the same politicians in elections. Also, we would all want to marry the same person, see the same movies, and spend time with the same friends. In reality, people are attracted to different types of people, places, and activities. One consequence of this fact is that you (and I) will never be liked by everyone.

Let's consider another example of how to challenge the thoughts that can trigger your social anxiety. Imagine that you are feeling nervous while giving a presentation. You are aware that, at times, your hands are shaking, and that your voice is a bit unsteady. Your automatic thought is that everyone will notice your anxiety, and that they will all think you don't know what you are talking about. How might you challenge these thoughts? What does the evidence tell you?

Here are some questions you might ask yourself to help you see the situation differently. First, how likely is it that everyone will notice your anxiety? Some people are so self-absorbed that they wouldn't notice anything about you unless you hit them over the head with it! If you don't believe this, try to get someone's attention in a public place; you will be surprised how difficult it can be sometimes.

Second, even if someone does notice your shaky hands and unsteady voice, what might that person think about you? Sure, the person may think you are incompetent. However, he or she might also think that you are simply nervous (as most people are while public speaking). It may help to remember, whenever you give a presentation, that for the people in the audience, your presentation is just a small part of their day, and a much smaller part of their lives. What is the likelihood that they are going to care that much whether your voice is unsteady?

Essentially, examining the evidence involves four basic steps: identifying your anxious thoughts, generating alternative beliefs, weighing the evidence supporting and contradicting your beliefs, and choosing more realistic beliefs. An example of how to use this strategy to deal with the anxiety about making small talk with a new neighbor is offered below:

1. **Identify the anxious thought.**

   - This person must think I'm stupid because I have nothing to say.

2. **Generate alternative beliefs.**

   - Perhaps he didn't notice that I was at a loss for words.

   - Although I didn't say much, neither did he. Maybe he is also shy.

   - Perhaps he thought I was simply preoccupied or in a hurry.

   - Perhaps he thought I am a bit shy, rather than thinking I'm stupid.

3. **Examine the evidence.**
   Evidence supporting my anxious belief:

   - In the past, I have had people mention that I tend to be quiet in social situations.

   - In high school I was teased a couple of times about being incompetent by people who didn't know me.

   Evidence supporting my alternative beliefs:

   - My new neighbor also seemed a bit uncomfortable.

   - It's perfectly normal for some conversations to be brief, and for people not to always have interesting things to say.

   - Even if he thought I was overly quiet, there is no reason to think that he would see that as a sign of stupidity. In fact, intelligence isn't really related to how much people talk. I know lots of people who talk a lot who don't seem all that bright to me.

4. **Choose a more realistic belief.**

- Perhaps my neighbor noticed that I was quiet, but it is extremely unlikely that he thought I am stupid.

Exercise: Evaluate the Evidence

Over the coming weeks, or for as long as you are working on using the strategies in this book, try going through these four steps to evaluate the evidence each time you experience anxious thoughts related to social situations (if possible, do this at least several times per week). Try doing the exercise on paper at first. Over time, the strategy will become easier to do in your head, and, eventually, it may become almost automatic.

COMBAT CATASTROPHIC THINKING

There is a simple and effective method to combat catastrophic thinking. Instead of thinking about how terrible and unmanageable it would be if your fearful thoughts were to come true, this strategy involves asking yourself questions such as:

- So what if my prediction comes true?
- How can I cope with that outcome if it does happen?
- Does this matter as much as I think it does?
- If my fearful prediction comes true, will it matter in the big scheme of things? Will it matter tomorrow? A month from now? In a year?

This strategy will help you to recognize that negative outcomes often don't matter nearly as much as you think they will. In the big picture, it really doesn't matter whether you sweat when you are on a date. In fact, it may not even matter if your date never wants to see you again. If anything, while dating, it would be unusual *not* to be rejected from time to time. Similarly, you can probably afford to lose your train of thought during a presentation, you can afford to be boring during a conversation, and you can afford to unintentionally offend a store clerk by trying to return an item that you purchased by mistake. All of these types of situations arise for most people from time to time. They are uncomfortable, but the consequences are usually minimal.

Exercise: Record and Measure Your Catastrophic Thoughts

Over the next few weeks, try to record examples of your catastrophic thinking in your journal. Are there times when you assume that a particular situation will become absolutely unmanageable? If so, try using some of the decatastrophizing questions provided above in the section entitled "Combat Catastrophic Thinking." Record your anxiety level (using a 0 to 100 point scale) before and after going through the exercise. Pay attention to any changes in your anxiety level.

SHIFTING PERSPECTIVES

Shifting perspectives is another powerful way of reducing social anxiety. If social anxiety is a problem for you, the chances are good that you are much harder on yourself than others are likely to be. You may also be much harder on yourself than you are on others. One way of viewing a situation more realistically is to try to think about the situation from the perspective of someone who doesn't have problems with social anxiety. Or, you may benefit from imagining what you would think about someone else who behaved the same way you behave in social situations. Here are some questions that you can use to jump-start the process of shifting perspectives:

- How might someone who isn't socially anxious (for example, my spouse) view this same situation?

- What would I say to a loved one who was having the anxious thought that I'm having?

- What questions would I encourage another person in my situation to ask (to challenge his or her anxious thoughts)?

- What would I think about another person who is sweating (or shaking, blushing, mixing up his or her words, etc.)? Would I assume all kinds of terrible things about that person?

- What would people think about someone other than me (e.g., my best friend) if they noticed her anxiety during a presentation? Would they think all the same terrible thoughts that I imagine they have about me during my presentations?

Exercise: Shift Your Perspective

Over the next few weeks, try to use perspective shifting when you experience thoughts about other people judging your performance in social situations. Record your anxiety level (using a 0 to 100 point scale) before and after working through the exercise. Pay attention to any changes in your anxiety level.

BEHAVIORAL EXPERIMENTS

This chapter has emphasized your need to learn to think like a scientist; that is, to consider all the evidence before deciding whether your anxious beliefs are true. Sometimes, though, you may not have all the evidence you need to reach a realistic conclusion. That's when behavioral experiments can be particularly important. This strategy involves testing out your predictions by conducting systematic research, just as a scientist would.

Instead of changing your thoughts by passively thinking about the situation, behavioral experiments require you to actually engage in some sort of behavior so you can learn through real experience whether your anxious thoughts are biased or exaggerated. Consider Randi's story below.

Randi, a thirty-three-year-old graphics designer, was in therapy to learn how to manage her social anxiety. Because of her fear of meeting new people, she hadn't had a date in years, and she often felt very lonely.

One day, Randi came to her therapy session feeling quite discouraged. She had just come from a busy coffee shop, and her experience there had confirmed her belief that she is an inadequate person. While in the coffee shop, she had noted that she was the only one who was there alone, and that everyone else in the coffee shop seemed happy. Her therapist wondered whether Randi might have been selectively paying attention only to the information that confirmed her anxious beliefs while ignoring any information that might support a more balanced view of the situation. Therefore, her therapist suggested that she should try the following experiment.

Randi was instructed to return to the same coffee shop immediately after the session, and to bring with her a pen and a piece of paper. Her assignment was to make a note of each person in the coffee shop, whether he or she was alone, and how happy each person seemed, using a scale ranging from -100 (very unhappy) to +100 (very happy).

When Randi returned to the coffee shop a second time, she did notice that, in fact, there were quite a few people there alone. In addition, although some people seemed to be very happy, a couple of people seemed quite unhappy, and for most people she couldn't really tell how happy they were. This experience was a powerful demonstration that the first time she'd been in the coffee shop she'd focused her attention on the other people there in a completely biased way.

There are many other types of behavioral experiments you might try. When designing an appropriate behavioral experiment, the question to ask yourself is "What can I do to discover whether my belief it true?" For example, if you are convinced that it would be terrible to be the center of attention, you could try doing things to draw attention to yourself (e.g., drop some books in a public place). If you are convinced that it would be a disaster to lose your train of thought during a presentation, try purposely losing your train of thought. Or, if you are worried that you must be entertaining during a conversation, try be dull on purpose and see what happens. Of course, use good judgment in designing your behavioral experiments. Don't do anything that would be likely get you into trouble. For example, don't call your boss an idiot just to see what might happen.

Exercise: Test and Record Your Anxious Beliefs

Over the next few weeks, create a series of small experiments to test out your anxious beliefs and predictions. In your journal, record your thoughts immediately before the experiment. After completing the experiment, record the outcome. What did the experiment teach you about the validity of your anxious beliefs?

Troubleshooting

As with most things in life, cognitive therapy doesn't always go smoothly. Here are some typical problems that people often encounter while trying to use the cognitive strategies described in this chapter, as well as some possible solutions.

Problem: Even though part of me recognizes that my anxious beliefs are exaggerated, it is hard for me to believe the alternative, "realistic" thoughts.

Solution: This problem often arises during cognitive therapy. At the beginning, the strategies may seem superficial or artificial. The solution is to keep at it. With practice, the more realistic alternative beliefs become stronger and more automatic. You may also find that the behavioral strategies, including behavioral experiments (in this chapter) and exposure (in chapter 4) are particularly effective for changing your anxious thoughts.

Problem: When I am anxious, I can't think clearly enough to challenge my beliefs.

Solution: If you are too anxious to use the cognitive strategies, then try using them when you're less anxious. For example, you can use them before entering a feared situation, or you can use them after the situation has ended.

Problem: I have no way of knowing whether my anxious beliefs are realistic.

Solution: If you have avoided a feared situation for many years, you may not have a good idea of what will actually happen if you risk confronting the situation. If this is the case, you may not be able to rely on your past experience to determine whether your beliefs are realistic. However, you will still benefit from seeking out experiences that provide you with the evidence you may be missing, including conducting behavioral experiments.

Problem: When I consider the evidence for my beliefs, I conclude that my anxious thoughts really are true.

Solution: In some cases, your anxious beliefs may be true. For example, some people who worry about being judged negatively by others are in fact ignored, teased, or disliked by others. Often, this occurs because individuals who are very shy sometimes do things that trigger a negative impression in others. Examples of such behaviors include avoiding intimacy, avoiding eye contact, standing far away, and speaking quietly. People who are very shy may come across as aloof, or even as snobbish, or very angry. If people are in fact judging you negatively, your treatment should focus on trying to identify why this is happening, and then on trying to change the behaviors that lead to negative reactions from others. See chapter 5 for a discussion on strategies for improving your interpersonal skills.

4

Confront Anxiety-Provoking Situations

In chapter 3, you learned about strategies to become more aware of your anxious beliefs and to replace them with more realistic interpretations and thoughts. Changing the way you view social situations is one of the most important factors for reducing your anxiety. In addition to the strategies from chapter 3 (such as questioning your beliefs, examining the evidence, and so on), another powerful way of changing anxious thinking is through direct exposure to feared situations. Unlike many of the cognitive strategies discussed in the previous chapter, exposure involves providing yourself with new experiences to prove that many of the thoughts contributing to your social anxiety are exaggerated, and perhaps untrue.

Can you think of a situation that once frightened you, but *that no longer is a problem*? For example, were you ever afraid of driving (perhaps when you first learned to drive), or of the dark, or of skiing for the first time? When you think back to the first time you met your spouse or your best friend, do you remember being anxious or nervous the first few times you got together? Almost everyone has situations that make them nervous or frightened; however, most of us also have managed to overcome at least one or two fears that were a problem in the past.

If you are able to think of a fear that once was a problem for you, how did you manage to overcome it? Why do you suppose you are no longer afraid? In many cases, people overcome their fears naturally when they decide to confront a feared situation despite the discomfort, perhaps in order to avoid problems at work, at school, or in relationships. With repeated practice, the fear tends to decrease.

In most cases, confronting situations that you fear excessively will lead over time to a reduction in your fear. Exposure appears to be an effective method for fear reduction across cultures, and psychologists who study animal behavior have found that exposure reduces fear behaviors in animals as well. This chapter provides an overview of how you can use the principles of exposure to overcome your own fears.

The Problem with Avoidance

When people are uncomfortable, nervous, or afraid, their natural tendency is to try to do whatever they can to feel better. If their fear is being triggered by a particular object or situation, the easiest way to get rid of the fear is to escape from the situation or to avoid the situation altogether. Each time people escape from a feared situation, they reinforce the idea that avoidance makes them feel better. So, it is not surprising that people who are shy or those who experience anxiety in social and performance situations tend to avoid the situations that arouse their fear.

Avoidance isn't necessarily a bad thing. Most people avoid situations from time to time. In fact, 77.8 percent of people in a recently published survey reported a strong desire to avoid a social situation, at least from time to time (Purdon et al. 2001). It is certainly not important to confront every situation, just because it makes you uncomfortable. If you don't enjoy roller coasters, you can probably afford to not ride on them without suffering any serious consequences.

However, avoidance can become a problem when it occurs frequently, when it leads to interference in a person's day-to-day life (for example, missed social opportunities, impaired functioning at work), or when a person's anxiety leads to significant problems in his or her life. In other words, if you experience significant shyness or social anxiety, to the point of it being a problem and interfering with your life, avoidance is definitely a habit to consider breaking. By beginning to confront feared situations, you will become more confident, you will learn that your worst fears don't come true, and, eventually, you will begin to experience lower levels of fear.

SAFETY BEHAVIORS AND SOCIAL ANXIETY

Avoidance can be much more subtle than simply escaping from a situation or refusing to enter a situation. Often, people find less-obvious ways to protect themselves from feeling anxious in social situations. Some examples of more subtle safety behaviors include:

- Drinking alcohol or using other drugs while in social situations.

- Distracting oneself from feelings of anxiety or from uncomfortable physical sensations (for example, trying to think pleasant thoughts in order to avoid noticing feelings of anxiety).

- Arriving at social gatherings early to get a "good" seat or to avoid being the center of attention once everyone is already there.

- Steering conversations toward "safe" topics (for example, asking another person questions to avoid having to talk about yourself).

- Socializing only with people who talk a lot, to avoid having to contribute much to the conversation yourself.

- Wearing heavy makeup or turtleneck tops to hide blushing on your face or neck.

- Socializing only in dimly lit places, so people won't notice your signs of anxiety.

- Finding out who is invited to a party before deciding whether to attend.

- Avoiding smiling or making eye contact for fear of triggering a conversation.

- Overpreparing your presentations to be absolutely sure that you don't make any mistakes.

- Completing checks before going to a store, to avoid having to write in front of the cashier.

- Always using the bathroom before leaving home, to ensure that there won't be the need to use a public bathroom.

- Avoiding activities that trigger feared symptoms, such as blushing, sweating, or shaking (for example, avoiding physical exertion in public, because exercise triggers sweating).

Like the more obvious forms of avoidance, subtle safety behaviors are often effective for reducing anxiety and fear in the short term. However, they help to maintain your anxiety in the long term because they prevent you from learning that the situation is safe. As you long as you engage in these safety behaviors, you are much more likely to believe that the only reason you survived relatively unscathed was because of these avoidance behaviors. So, as part of exposing yourself to feared situations, it will be important to begin to eliminate many of the small things that you do to keep your anxiety in check. A number of controlled studies have demonstrated clearly that eliminating safety behaviors, along with exposing oneself to feared situations, leads to significantly more improvement during treatment of excessive social anxiety, compared to exposure alone (Morgan and Raffle 1999; Wells et al. 1995).

Exercise: List Your Safety Behaviors

In your journal, make a list of the safety behaviors that that you tend to use in social situations. What happens when you don't use these behaviors?

Planning for Exposure Therapy

Before beginning to use exposure, a bit of planning will be useful. Specifically, you will need to have a good understanding of (1) the specific situations that you tend to avoid and the situations that trigger your anxiety, (2) the factors that influence your fear in these situations, and (3) the subtle ways in which you avoid these situations. You may already have generated a list of feared situations (see the exercise called "Rate the Situations That Are Uncomfortable for You" in chapter 2) and a list of subtle avoidance behaviors (see the exercise entitled "List Your Safety Behaviors" earlier in this chapter). What you have not have done yet is to generate a list of variables that affect your fear level in social situations. The exercise at the end of this section asks you to do just that.

People's anxiety tends to vary in severity depending on many different factors. For example, certain aspects of the people with whom you interact may affect your fear level. Perhaps you find it more difficult to interact with others who are your own age than with others who are much older or younger. Or, perhaps certain aspects of the other person's personality (for example, how aggressive, assertive, confident, or intelligent the other person is) affect your level of comfort. Other features that can affect your comfort level may include the sex of the other individual, how well you know that person, whether he or she is married or in a relationship, and whether you find that person physically attractive. Particular aspects of the situation also may affect your fear level, including the lighting, the number of other people present, whether you are sitting or standing, what you are wearing, and whether you are the focus of attention, versus being just one individual among a crowd of people.

Exercise: List the Variables That Affect Your Level of Anxiety

Pick up your journal and, on a fresh page, create a list of all the variables you can think of that frequently affect the level of fear or anxiety you experience in the social situations that tend to make you uncomfortable.

Developing an Exposure Hierarchy

Once you've identified the types of situations that make you uncomfortable, the variables that affect your level of anxiety in these situations, and the types of safety (or avoidance) behaviors you normally use to cope with these situations, the next step is to develop an exposure hierarchy. An exposure hierarchy is a list of feared situations, ordered by rank from the most difficult (at the top) to the least difficult (at the bottom). The hierarchy is used to guide an individual's exposure practices.

Typically, people begin by practicing with the items near the bottom of their hierarchy, over and over again, until the items no longer trigger anxiety. Then they move up to the more difficult items in a step-by-step fashion until eventually most, if not all, of the items on the list can be practiced with little anxiety. When developing your own hierarchy, here are a few guidelines to keep in mind:

- Try to generate between ten and fifteen items.

- Select items that are practical (though challenging). For example, if it's unlikely that you will ever have an opportunity to meet the Queen of England, listing "Meeting the Queen" as one of your hierarchy items is not such a great idea. Choose situations that come up from time to time, or that you could arrange if you wanted to.

- Make the items as specific as possible. Specify the location, who is there, and any other factors that are likely to influence your fear level.

- If your anxiety occurs in a wide range of social situations, you may consider developing more than one hierarchy. For example, you could have one hierarchy for situations involving being the center of attention (such as public speaking) and another hierarchy for situations involving interpersonal contact with others (such as dating or initiating conversations).

- Don't concern yourself with whether you feel ready to try all the items on your exposure hierarchy. At first, the chances are good that you will be able to try the items on the bottom half. Initially, the top few items may seem impossible.

Here is a sample exposure hierarchy for someone who experiences anxiety in most social and performance situations. Note that in addition to listing feared situations in their order of difficulty, a hierarchy usually includes ratings (using a scale from 0 to 100) that reflect the extent to which the person fears each situation (0 = no fear, and 100 = maximum fear).

From time to time, it's useful to rerate your hierarchy items as a way of measuring the changes in your fear levels.

SAMPLE HIERARCHY

Situation	Fear Rating
Throw a party at my home and invite everyone from work, and avoid drinking any alcohol.	100
Attend a party with my spouse at a coworker's home, and avoid having any alcohol.	90
Attend the opening of an art show and make casual conversation with other attendees without drinking any alcohol.	90
Invite another couple (Kevin and Katie) over for dinner at our home.	85
Have lunch with a coworker and a third person whom I don't know well.	80
Arrive at my night class a few minutes late, so all my classmates stare at me when I walk in to take my seat.	70
Invite another couple (Kevin and Katie) for dinner in a restaurant.	70
Make small talk (e.g., about the weather) with strangers on an elevator.	60
Tell my coworkers about my weekend when arriving at work on Monday morning.	55
Eat lunch at my desk, with others watching.	50
Fill out a form at the bank with others watching.	35
Ask for directions at a gas station.	30
Drop my keys in a public place where people are likely to notice.	25

Exercise: Create Your Exposure
Hierarchy

In your journal, on a fresh page (or pages),
develop your own personal exposure hierarchy
based on the guidelines presented in the section
you just finished reading.

Guidelines for Exposure Therapy

In all likelihood, you have had some negative experiences in
social situations. You've probably made social blunders of various kinds, and you probably have embarrassed yourself. These
negative experiences in social situations may have strengthened
your belief that the best thing to do is avoid contact with other
people whenever possible. If that is so, you may be asking
yourself, "How is exposure to social situations going to help
me overcome my fear if it hasn't helped in the past?" If anything, it may seem as if your past exposures to social situations
have only strengthened your fear.

There are important differences between the types of exposure you may have had in the past and the types of exposure that
have proved to be useful for overcoming problems with anxiety
and fear. In the past, chances are that your exposures were usually unpredictable, brief, and infrequent. Furthermore, you may
not have had have the tools (such as the cognitive strategies
described in chapter 3, or the other techniques described
throughout this book) to deal effectively with the feared situations. You also may have overrelied on your safety behaviors to
combat your uncomfortable feelings (for example, having several
glasses of wine upon arriving at a party).

As it turns out, exposures that are brief, infrequent, and
unpredictable are not especially helpful, and may even lead to
a worsening of fear. What you tell yourself during exposures

can also affect the outcome, and fighting your fear only seems to make things worse.

For exposure to be effective, the following guidelines should be followed.

EXPOSURES SHOULD BE PREDICTABLE AND UNDER YOUR CONTROL. It's really amazing how different if feels to enter a feared situation with the perspective of someone purposely choosing to enter that situation, versus someone who is forced to enter the feared situation. Remember, you are in control of the situation, and you are entering the situation by choice. Also, predictable exposure appears to be more useful than unpredictable exposure. So, it is a good idea to plan your practices in advance, so you know when they are going to take place.

It is also helpful to anticipate the possible outcomes and how you might handle them. For example, if you intend to practice talking to strangers on elevators, be prepared for some people to respond positively, others to respond negatively, and some to not respond at all. By preparing yourself for a possible negative outcome, you will be less shocked if and when it happens.

EXPOSURES SHOULD BE PROLONGED. If you leave the situation after just a few minutes, you will only reinforce your belief that the best way to reduce your discomfort is to avoid the situation and leave. If you stay for a longer time (e.g., for an hour or two), you will learn that your discomfort eventually decreases, even if you don't leave. If a situation is inherently brief, it is best to practice it over and over again, until your fear diminishes. For example, if you are fearful of asking others for information, try standing in the mall for an hour or more and asking dozens of different people what time it is.

EXPOSURES SHOULD BE FREQUENT. When people don't benefit from exposure, often that's because they haven't followed this guideline. Exposure simply won't work if it doesn't take place often enough. To get the benefit, you must practice whenever the opportunity arises. If the opportunity doesn't arise, you need to create opportunities. It's generally recommended that people practice some form of exposure (for at least an hour, and preferably more) almost daily. Practices occurring at least four or five times a week will generally lead to a reduction of fear over a period of a few weeks or months.

DON'T FIGHT YOUR FEAR. Fighting your fear just makes it worse. By just letting the fear happen (and giving yourself permission to experience all the different sensations that you feel when you're anxious), your level of fear will come down much more quickly. Even if you blush, shake, or sweat in front of others, just let it happen. Lots of people experience these feelings (see the section entitled "Exposure to Anxiety-Provoking Sensations" in this chapter) and most people make no special effort to fight or hide these symptoms.

ELIMINATE SAFETY BEHAVIORS. This is just a reminder—in addition to exposing yourself to feared situations, it is also important to begin to decrease your use of safety behaviors. At the start, it may be too difficult to eliminate them completely. If so, you can let go of them gradually, as you become more comfortable.

TAKE STEPS GRADUALLY, BUT TRY TO KEEP THINGS MOVING. If a particular practice is too difficult, try something easier. There is nothing wrong with taking steps gradually, as long as you keep forging ahead. There are, however, a couple of disadvantages of going too slowly. First, your progress will be slower if you practice things that are very easy, or if you move though your hierarchy very slowly. Second, if your progress is too slow, you may start to lose your motivation for the treatment and give up before making all the gains that you might have made if you had kept going. In contrast, the biggest risk when moving too quickly is that you will feel more uncomfortable. You'll need to decide what is the best pace for you to take, and how much discomfort you are willing to experience along the way.

PRACTICE EXPOSURE WITH DIFFERENT PEOPLE, AND IN DIFFERENT SETTINGS. It is useful to build in some variety to your practices. For example, if you are nervous eating with other people, it's useful to practice eating with different types of people (for example, friends, coworkers, and strangers), and in different types of places (for example, casual restaurants, food courts, nice restaurants, the cafeteria at work, or at your home). Practicing in different types of situations will lead to more complete improvement in your symptoms and may help to prevent your anxiety from returning later on.

BE PREPARED FOR SETBACKS. Unfortunately, progress is rarely smooth. You are likely to have some exposures that are better than you expected, and others that are worse. You may have days when your physical symptoms are particularly strong, or days when the people with whom you are interacting are not especially warm. Try not to feel discouraged when a practice doesn't go well. Over time, the percentage of positive experiences will increase and the percentage of negative practices will decrease.

DON'T TRY TO BE PERFECT. Exposure practices are not about trying to make a perfect impression on others. Along the way, you may be judged by others, and you may even make a complete fool of yourself (just like everyone else does from time to time). Use the exposures as opportunities to take social risks, to try new things, and to learn more about how others respond to the things you do. If you make a mistake along the way, try to let it go. If perfectionism tends to create problems for you, the strategies discussed in chapter 10 will be especially useful.

EXPECT TO FEEL ANXIOUS. A common mistake that people often make during exposure practices is to believe that they should be able to do the practice without getting anxious. If they feel fear, or if they sweat, shake, or blush, they may feel disappointed in themselves, as if they've somehow failed. If you are one of those people, it's time to change your expectations. You are supposed to feel anxious during exposure practices, and you are supposed to feel the symptoms that you experience when you are nervous. An ideal practice is one in which you experience fear and you stick with it, ideally long enough for the fear to decrease. If you don't experience fear during an exposure practice, it probably wasn't difficult enough.

PLAN YOUR EXPOSURE PRACTICES IN ADVANCE. It is best to decide up front what practices you intend to do and when you will do them, rather than deciding at the last minute based on how you feel. It is important to practice exposure even on the days when you feel more anxious. One useful strategy is to schedule your exposure practices at the start of each week, for the next seven days.

COMBAT NEGATIVE THINKING WITH COGNITIVE STRATEGIES. Your exposure practices will not be as helpful as they could be if immediately after an exposure you review all the reasons why the exposure didn't go well, how you made a fool of yourself, and how you are convinced that others are thinking terrible things about you. If your tendency is to think the worst in social situations, try using the cognitive strategies discussed in chapter 3 to help combat negative thinking before starting an exposure practice, during the practice, and after the practice has ended.

Exposure to Anxiety-Provoking Situations

Now that you understand how exposure practices should be conducted, and you have generated your personal hierarchy, you are ready to start confronting the situations you fear. It's essential to think of exposure as an ongoing process. Just reading this chapter and trying a few exposure practices won't lead to significant change. Like physical exercise, exposure-based exercise requires frequent, ongoing practice. Early on, more frequent practice is needed, but once your anxiety levels have decreased, occasional exposure practice should be enough to maintain your gains.

Here are a number of ideas for possible exposure practices that you may find useful for dealing with fears of particular types of social situations. Note that if a particular exposure is just too difficult, you may want to start with a simulated or role-playing exposure. For example, if interviewing for real jobs seems too frightening, start by doing some practice interviews with friends or family members. When those become easier, then try going on a real interview.

PUBLIC SPEAKING AND PERFORMING

If you have opportunities to speak in public, take advantage of them. Such practices may include speaking up in meetings, asking questions in class or at a public lecture, giving presentations at work, or giving toasts at parties or dinners. If these opportunities don't arise naturally, you may need to make them happen. Volunteer to speak to a group of students at a local school about your work. Or, take a drama, music, or public speaking course. Many people also benefit from joining Toastmasters, a self-help organization where members help one another to improve their public speaking skills during weekly meetings. It is fairly inexpensive to join. For more information about Toastmasters, check out their Web site, www.toastmasters.org.

CASUAL SOCIAL CONTACT AND SMALL TALK

Opportunities for casual social contact probably come up every day—you just need to start taking advantage of them. If making small talk in groups is too difficult, start with briefer social contacts, such as asking for the time or for directions in a public place, like a mall. Or, you can practice saying hello to people in line at the bus stop, on an elevator, or in other public places. Chatting with coworkers when you first arrive at work and going for lunch with friends or acquaintances are also ideal opportunities for casual conversation. Other options include attending social events (e.g., community dances, art gallery openings, class reunions, holiday parties), talking to other dog owners when you are out walking your dog, or having friends over for dinner.

At first, you may feel as if you have nothing to say. As your anxiety decreases, it will likely become much easier. Remember, the purpose of these exposures is not to be entertaining and witty. The purpose is to help you to feel more comfortable in social situations. If you also happen to be entertaining and witty, that's an added bonus. Chapters 5 and 7 also have ideas to help you with anxiety about making small talk.

DEALING WITH CONFLICT AND THE POSSIBILITY OF UPSETTING OTHERS

From time to time everyone confronts difficult situations with others. People who are shy or socially anxious often prefer to avoid these situations. It isn't recommended that you purposely treat other people badly or that you purposely do things to upset them. However, it seems reasonable to consider standing up for your rights when the likely consequences are minimal and you have little to lose, even if there is a small chance that someone else might become upset.

Examples might include sending a bad meal back in a restaurant, returning an item to a store, asking a noisy neighbor to be quiet after 10 P.M., questioning an error on a bill, or doing multiple transactions at a bank machine, even when there is a long line behind you waiting to use the machine. As a general rule, don't do things that will get you into trouble. For example, don't tell you boss that you can't stand him or her. Don't complain to your noisy neighbor if he or she has a history of being violent or is the type of person who most people would find scary. In other words, when designing your exposure practices, use your common sense.

BEING THE CENTER OF ATTENTION

If just being in public is difficult for you, then exposure practices should include spending time around others. Depending on the content of your fear, practices might involve walking down a busy street, working out in a gym, shopping in a crowded mall, seeing a movie or play at a crowded theater, having a snack in a café or restaurant, reading in a library, or just sitting on your front porch watching people walk past. If your fear is of having all eyes focused on you, then doing something to draw the attention of others would be appropriate. Examples of possible exposure practices include such things as dropping your keys, calling out to another person from across a crowded room, spilling a glass of water, having your mobile phone or pager go off in a public place, purposely pronouncing a word incorrectly, or wearing a piece of clothing inside out. If none of these practices gets the attention of others, then perhaps nothing will.

EATING OR DRINKING IN FRONT OF OTHERS

Exposures involving eating in front of others should take into account such variables as the setting (eating at home, in a fancy restaurant, or in a casual setting like a food court; eating in a well-lit versus dark room), the people with whom you are eating (strangers, acquaintances, close friends), the types of food being eaten (finger foods versus those eaten with utensils; hot foods versus cold foods), and any other factors that are likely to affect your fear. The possibilities are endless, ranging from eating a packet of raisins at your desk to dining out for five-course meal in a formal restaurant with a large group of people. As with all exposures, start with moderately difficult practices and work up to the more difficult ones when your fear has decreased.

WRITING IN FRONT OF OTHERS

For many people, the fear of writing in front of others is related to the fear of having others notice their unsteady hands. For other people, it is a fear of having others think badly about their handwriting, spelling, or the content of what they are writing. Regardless of the reason for the fear, the key to overcoming it is to write in front of others. Try filling out forms in a public place, write a letter in a café or on a bus, or practice writing checks in front of cashiers. (Note that writing many small checks for one or two items each will give you more practice than writing one big check for a large number of items.) If you are fearful of having unsteady hands, try purposely making your hands shake. The worst thing that can happen is that other people will know you have shaky hands. But people frequently have unsteady hands for all sorts of reasons, and many of them are not in the least bit concerned if other people notice their hands are shaking.

JOB INTERVIEWS

If you need to look for a job, but the thought of interviewing is overwhelming, the best thing you can do is to exposure yourself to situations that resemble job interviews. Perhaps you can start with simulated interviews with friends, or friends of friends (that's because this exposure practice is more effective if you do it with people whom you don't know). You can also apply for a large number of jobs that don't interest you. Interviews for jobs that you don't really want will give you the practice you need without the pressure of having to make a good impression on the person interviewing you.

DEALING WITH AUTHORITY FIGURES

If dealing with authority figures is anxiety provoking, try making a point of having some contact with people in authority. For some people, this might include scheduling meetings with their boss, making casual conversation with a supervisor, meeting with a bank manager to discuss a loan, discussing a problem with a family physician, or having an extended conversation with a college professor. The practices you select should be based on the particular types of authority figures who trigger your anxiety.

Exposure to Anxiety-Provoking Sensations

The previous section reviewed strategies for exposing oneself to feared situations. However, people who experience high levels of social anxiety are fearful not only of saying the wrong thing or of looking stupid; often they are also fearful of showing any sign of their anxiety and of having others notice their anxiety symptoms.

In reality, on occasion, almost everyone experiences some physical symptoms of anxiety in social situations. My colleagues and I recently published a survey of college students in which we asked how frequently participants experienced various physical symptoms of anxiety in social situations (Purdon et al. 2001). Of the eighty-one people we surveyed, 73 percent reported excessive sweating in social situations from time to time, 58 percent reported having shaky hands and knees, 75 percent reported occasional blushing, and 59.3 percent reported at least sometimes having an unsteady voice in public. Several of the other symptoms that were reported by most individuals included heart palpitations (71.6 percent), stammering (56.8 percent), and trouble expressing themselves (81.5 percent).

So, if you experience symptoms such as these, you are not alone. In the long term, trying to prevent these symptoms will only maintain your fear of having them. In other words, as long as you are fearful of experiencing uncomfortable sensations, you are much more likely to continue experiencing them in the future. The best way to combat your fear of these feelings is to purposely expose yourself to the sensations. Here are some examples of exposure practices that might help to decrease your fear of anxiety-provoking sensations:

- For the fear of sweating in front of others, try purposely bringing on sweating in social situations. Run around the block before going into a party. Or, wear a warm sweater while giving a presentation.

- For the fear of blushing in front of others, try rubbing your face before entering a social situation. Eat hot foods, or wear a bit of blush (makeup). Tensing the muscles of your body with exercise can also cause your face to become red.

- If you are fearful of shaking in front of others, try purposely shaking while eating, holding a glass, or while writing.

- To overcome the fear of losing your train of thought during presentations, try purposely to seem as though you have forgotten your place while speaking in a meeting or while giving a toast.

Exercises such as these will help you to recognize that the consequences of experiencing any of the physical symptoms of anxiety are usually minimal.

Troubleshooting

If you are practicing exposures as they are described throughout this chapter, you should experience a reduction in your fear and anxiety. However, the road to feeling less fear may be a bumpy one. Here are a few problems that people sometimes encounter during exposure therapy, as well as some possible solutions.

Problem: I can't seem to get around to practicing exposure. I just seem to be too busy.

Solution: Try scheduling the exposure practices the way you would schedule appointments, classes, or any other activities in your life. If you are concerned about forgetting to practice, set an alarm to remind you when it is time to do your homework. If you are overly busy, you can piggyback your exposures onto other activities that you need to do in any case. For example, instead of eating lunch alone, plan to eat lunch with someone else. If all else fails, carve out the time you need to do the exposures. Take a few days off from work and pack those days with activities that provide you with opportunities to confront feared situations.

Problem: I'm too frightened to do my exposure homework.

Solution: If a particular practice is too difficult, the solution is simple. Try something easier. You can always work your way up to the more difficult practices later.

Problem: My fear doesn't seem to lessen during my exposure practices.

Solution: There are several possible reasons why your fear level may stay high. First, fear doesn't always decrease at each and every practice. Try the same exposure exercise on another day. You may have better luck then. In some cases, when the fear stays high, that may be a sign that (1) you are ruminating about any negative consequences that may occur, (2) you are overrelying on safety behaviors, or

(3) you are trying something that is too difficult. Remember to use the cognitive coping strategies to manage negative thinking. Try not to use safety behaviors and other forms of subtle avoidance. Finally, if a particular situation is completely overwhelming, try something easier.

5

Change the Way You Communicate and Improve Your Relationships

Most of the time, people who are worried about looking bad in front of others actually come across very well, and they perform much better than they think. Still, for some individuals, and in certain situations, people who are particularly shy may not present themselves in the best possible light. There are several reasons for this. First, by avoiding social situations for many years, some people never got the opportunity to master the communication skills they needed to deal effectively with others. Just like learning to drive, mastering the art of social interaction requires practice. For example, without previous experience interviewing for jobs, it's unlikely that a person will perform brilliantly during his or her first interview.

A second reason why social anxiety is sometimes associated with poor performance is due to the anxiety itself, which may detract from an individual's ability to perform as effectively as he or she would like. For example, if your heart is pounding during a presentation, you may lose track of your train of thought because your attention may be focused almost exclusively on your chest.

Third, some of the subtle avoidance strategies and safety behaviors that individuals use to manage their anxiety (e.g., standing far away from others, avoiding eye contact, speaking quietly) sometimes may be perceived by others as a sign of discomfort, aloofness, anger, or social awkwardness, which may lead people to respond differently than they might have otherwise. In other words, the things you do to avoid having others respond negatively sometimes can lead to the very response you are trying desperately to prevent.

Chances are good that with repeated exposure to the feared social situations, and with repeated efforts to challenge your anxious thinking, you will become more comfortable. As a result, your performance will also improve. In other words, to improve your social and communication skills, you probably don't need to do anything more than just practice using the strategies described in chapters 3 and 4.

Still, learning some pointers regarding effective communication can help to fine-tune your social interaction skills. This chapter will provide suggestions for how to stop engaging in anxious behaviors that increase the likelihood of negative judgments from others.

As you work through the chapter, keep in mind that no matter how great your social skills are, they will never be perfect. Like everyone, from time to time, you will continue to stumble, and you will occasionally make a bad impression on another person. Fortunately, it is not important for you to perform perfectly in every situation; in fact, it's impossible to perform perfectly in every situation. Social behaviors that are effective in one situation are ineffective in others, depending on many factors, including the values, expectations, life experiences, and cultural backgrounds of the people with whom you interact. For example, the ideal way to ask one person out on a date may completely backfire if used with someone else.

There are many different aspects of communication that can be influenced by social anxiety, including a person's performance during job interviews, public speaking, dating, negotiating, dealing with conflict, and making casual conversation. Because of space limitations, this chapter will emphasize skills in two areas: nonverbal communication (including body language, eye contact, and other aspects) and making conversation. For more information about improving communication skills, two excellent books are *Messages: The Communication Skills Book* (McKay, Davis, and Fanning 1995) and *People Skills*, by Robert Bolton (1979). There are also a number of excellent books on developing skills in more-specific areas, including dating (Browne 1997; Kuriansky 1999; Tessina 1998), making conversation (Garner 1997; Honeychurch and Watrous 2003)), mastering job interviews (Dorio 2000; Kennedy 2000; Stein 2003), being more assertive (Fleming 1997; Paterson 2000), and giving effective presentations (Bowman 1998; Buchan 1997; Davidson 2003; Kushner 1996).

Nonverbal Communication

When we think about communication, many of us tend to think mostly about the words we use to communicate a message. However, a large component of what we communicate is nonverbal, relying instead on such things as facial expressions, tone of voice, and body language. That's why e-mail messages can be so easily misinterpreted. E-mail typically excludes the nonverbal cues that help us to understand a message's meaning. Therefore, it is easy to misinterpret a joke as a put-down or negative comment. Thank goodness for the smiley face [:-)] and the other annoying symbols that help to provide nonverbal messages when we communicate in cyberspace.

People who are shy or who feel anxious often engage in behaviors to minimize the intensity and duration of their interactions with others. In other words, they try *not to communicate*, in order to avoid being judged negatively. Of course, it is impossible to not communicate. Even if you completely avoid parties or meetings, you communicate a message to the people who expect to see you there. For example, others may interpret your frequent absences from meetings as a sign that you are shy, forgetful, lazy, or busy, or that you don't enjoy the company of your coworkers. In addition to complete avoidance, some more subtle nonverbal behaviors that are often associated with social anxiety include:

- Avoiding eye contact

- Smiling excessively

- Not smiling at all

- Speaking very quietly

- Speaking very quickly

- Appearing to be restless or in a hurry (for example, pacing or fidgeting)

- Standing or leaning away from others

- Crossing one's arms or legs

In many cases, these nonverbal behaviors communicate the message "stay away" even when the words you speak are saying something very different. Not surprisingly, other people tend to respond to these behaviors by being more aloof and less warm and friendly. Alternative behaviors (such as making appropriate eye contact, standing at an appropriate distance, talking at a volume that others can hear, maintaining a more open stance, smiling appropriately) are much more likely to lead to a positive response from others.

Exercise: Record and Experiment
with Your Nonverbal Behavior

Do you tend to have an anxious style of communicating nonverbally? In your journal, record
some of the ways in which your nonverbal communication may lead to negative responses from
others. Then, over the following week, try varying the way in which you communicate
nonverbally. For example, try varying the
amount of eye contact you engage in during
interactions with others, and pay attention to
their responses. Are store clerks friendlier when
you smile and make more eye contact than
when you avoid eye contact and maintain a
stone-cold expression on your face? Record the
outcomes of these experiments in your journal.

Conversation Skills

People often struggle to find things to say when making casual
conversation, especially if they are feeling anxious or uncomfortable. They may also end the conversation too early, or try
desperately to keep the conversation going long after it has run
out of steam. Anxiety may even lead people to talk too much,
which can lead to a negative impression on others. Below are
some common issues that arise in the context of making conversation, and some suggestions for how to deal more effectively with these situations when they occur.

STRIKING UP CONVERSATIONS

Although starting up conversations may seem difficult, it
tends to become easier with practice. Take advantage of
opportunities as they arise, in public places (for example, the

grocery store line), at work, and at social gatherings. If opportunities to practice don't come up, you can create them by surrounding yourself with other people. For example, take a course and practice talking to the other students in the class.

Conversations usually begin with a comment or topic that is not too personal, especially if you don't know the other individual well. You can start with a statement (e.g., it's cold in here), a question (e.g., how was traffic on your way to work?), or a compliment (e.g., your dog is adorable). Other possible topics might include your hobbies, something that recently happened to you, books you've read, current events, or sports. The longer you have known the other person, the more appropriate it is to discuss more personal topics, such as your relationships or values.

People who are shy sometimes avoid talking about themselves. They may steer conversations to focus instead on the other individual (for instance, by asking lots of questions). For most people, conversations are more interesting if information flows in both directions. Therefore, if you find yourself avoiding talking about yourself, try to volunteer more personal information. For example, discuss how your weekend went. Share your thoughts about a recent movie you saw. Often, people will respond positively when given the opportunity to find out more about you.

OPEN- AND CLOSED-ENDED QUESTIONS

If you do ask the other person some questions, try to ask open-ended questions, instead of closed-ended questions. A closed-ended question is one that usually leads to a one- or two-word answer, like yes, no, or fine. Examples of closed-ended questions include:

- How was your weekend?

- Do you like your salad?

- What do you do for a living?

In contrast, open-ended questions are questions that require a more detailed response. Generally, open-ended questions are more likely to keep a conversation interesting. Examples of open-ended questions include:

- What did you do this weekend?

- Tell me about your salad.

- What's it like working at the bank?

LEARNING TO LISTEN

Improving your conversation skills requires not only that you practice speaking with other people, but also that you practice listening to others. However, anxiety sometimes can make it difficult to listen. A couple of common blocks to listening include:

- Practicing how you intend to respond to what the other person is saying, instead of paying attention to the message he or she is trying to communicate

- Listening selectively to what the other person is saying; for example, focusing on the other person's comments that confirm your fear that he or she finds you boring (e.g., "I am very tired. I need to get going") and ignoring the more positive statements that same person makes ("I had a really nice time tonight, we should get together again")

Try to pay attention to the entire message being communicated by the other person. Also, it's useful to let the other person know that you are listening. Making eye contact, following up on the person's comments with a question, or asking for clarification when part of the person's message is unclear will communicate to that person that you are interested in what he or she is saying.

EXCESSIVE APOLOGIZING AND REASSURANCE SEEKING

A hallmark feature of social anxiety is the belief that one is coming across poorly, is unattractive or boring, or even that one is offensive to others. Not surprisingly, people who are shy sometimes apologize excessively, and, in some cases, may frequently seek reassurance from others to confirm that they are liked, that their performance was adequate, or that others find them attractive. There is nothing wrong with apologizing when you have done something wrong. Nor is there anything wrong with occasionally seeking reassurance. However, when these strategies are overused, they can have a negative impact on relationships. Nobody appreciates being apologized to for something that, in their mind, is not a problem. Similarly, it can feel like a burden when someone constantly needs and asks for reassurance in a friendship or other relationship.

ENDING CONVERSATIONS

People who are socially anxious often make one of two mistakes when it comes to ending conversations. Either they end the conversation too early (in order to escape from the situation), or they try desperately to keep the conversation going, long after it probably should have ended. If you tend to escape from conversations, try to stay in them longer. Over time, it will get easier to come up with things to talk about, and it will be easier to tolerate uncomfortable pauses.

If you feel responsible for keeping the conversation going forever, remember that even the best conversations come to an end, usually because, eventually, they become less interesting. For many of us, small talk is not particularly engaging, entertaining, or stimulating for more than a brief period. Perhaps that's why it's called "small talk." Often a conversation ends after a few minutes, sometimes less, and sometimes more. People have all sorts of ways in which they get out of conversations (for example, "I'll let you go," or "I am going to get another drink"). It is not a personal failure if you allow a conversation to end. That's part of the normal life cycle of every conversation.

Exercise: Break Out of Your Old Patterns

The next time you have the opportunity to engage in casual conversation, try breaking some of your normal patterns. If you tend to speak too little about yourself, try speaking more. If you feel responsible for keeping a conversation entertaining, try being less entertaining and see what happens. In short, try to be more flexible in conversations. Take more social risks. If a particular tactic seems to work well, practice using it in other situations. Record any changes you make, as well as the outcome (that is, others' responses) in your journal.

6

Medications

As stated in chapter 1, people with extreme levels of shyness and social anxiety may suffer from a problem known as social anxiety disorder (or social phobia). Researchers have identified a number of useful approaches for treating social anxiety disorder, including cognitive and behavioral treatments (see chapters 3, 4, and 5) and medications. Although, typically, medications are not used for mild levels of shyness or social anxiety, they are often effective for individuals with social anxiety disorder. In fact, psychological approaches and medications are about equally effective (especially in the short term) for treating this problem (Antony and McCabe 2003). This chapter reviews the use of medications for social anxiety disorder.

Should You Consider Taking Medications?

Before deciding whether medications are right for you, it's important to review the advantages and disadvantages of taking medications for social anxiety disorder.

ADVANTAGES OF MEDICATION TREATMENT

- Medications work. Most people who take appropriate medications for their social anxiety report a reduction in their symptoms. Although their social anxiety often doesn't disappear completely, the improvement experienced following treatment with medication is often significant.

- Medications are relatively easy to obtain. Any physician (for example, a family doctor or a psychiatrist) can prescribe medications, and in some states professionals from other fields may also be allowed to prescribe medications.

- Medications are easy to use. All you need to do is to remember to take your pill.

- Medications may work more quickly than other approaches, including cognitive and behavioral approaches. For example, the antidepressant medications discussed in this chapter usually work within a month, and certain other medications work even more quickly. In contrast, psychological treatments usually take a couple of months before significant benefits are noticed.

- Medications are often less expensive than psychological treatments, particularly over the short term. Although medications can be expensive, the weekly cost of psychotherapy sessions is often higher. However, the cost of medication adds up over time, so in the long term, medications may be more expensive than brief psychological treatment.

DISADVANTAGES OF MEDICATION TREATMENT

- All medications have possible side effects. Often, the side effects are mild and many people don't find them to be all that difficult to tolerate. Depending on the medication, side effects may improve after the first few weeks. Also, if one medication is too difficult to tolerate, often another one can be found with fewer side effects for that person.

- Medications are effective while an individual is taking them, but not necessarily after the drug has been stopped. Relapse rates tend to be higher upon stopping medication than upon stopping psychological treatment. Therefore, in the long term, cognitive and behavioral treatments (either alone or in combination with medication) are generally most effective.

- Because medications often need to be continued over years to obtain continued benefit, over the long term they tend to be more expensive than psychological treatments, which often last only a few months.

- Medications for social anxiety may interact with other medications, or with alcohol and recreational drugs. Some medications also may affect symptoms from various medical illnesses (for example, increasing the likelihood of high blood pressure or seizures in those who are vulnerable to experiencing these problems). Taking certain medications also may be dangerous while pregnant or breast-feeding. In light of these potential complications, medications should be taken only under a doctor's care. (In other words, don't try to save yourself a trip to the doctor by taking your sister's antidepressants.)

- Certain medications are difficult to discontinue because the effects of withdrawing from the medication may be unpleasant.

Some people really struggle with the decision of whether or not to take medication. They may believe that taking medication is a sign of weakness, or that the medication may lead to a permanent negative change that cannot be reversed. Neither belief is true. People from all walks of life take medications for a wide range of problems. Also, as far as we know, appropriate use of medications for anxiety generally will not lead to any permanent changes in your functioning or health. If you experience side effects, they will subside when the medication is stopped.

If you have easy access to both medications and cognitive behavioral therapy, then either approach, or a combination of these approaches, is likely to be useful. If you choose the "wrong" approach to treatment, you won't have lost much. For example, if a particular medication is not for you, you can always try a different medication, cognitive behavioral treatment, or no treatment at all. In other words, you are not stuck with your decision.

Choosing among Medication Options

So, you've decided to try medication. Which one should you try? Only three medications (all antidepressants) have the official stamp of approval from the U.S. Food and Drug Administration (FDA) for treating social anxiety disorder. These are paroxetine (Paxil), and more recently venlafaxine (Effexor XR) and sertraline (Zoloft). However, there are a number of other medications that also have been found to be effective for treating this problem. Although they may not be officially approved for social anxiety disorder, all of the medications reviewed in this chapter are approved for other related problems (for example, for other anxiety disorders, such as depression), and their safety is well established (Hofmann and Barlow 2002; Roy-Byrne and Cowley 2002).

Many factors go into deciding whether a medication receives FDA approval, including the evidence for the drug's safety and effectiveness, and whether the manufacturer of the drug decides to market the product for a given disorder. Your doctor's decision to prescribe a specific medication for your anxiety should take into account all of the research on the drug's effectiveness and safety, and not just whether the drug has been approved by the FDA for social anxiety disorder.

Other factors that are likely to influence which medication your doctor prescribes will include (1) the types of symptoms you experience; (2) the side effects associated with the various medication options; (3) your previous responses to medication; (4) previous responses by your close family members to various medications; (5) the cost of the medications; (6) possible interactions between the medication you are considering taking and other medications like herbal remedies, and illnesses; (7) whether you tend to drink alcohol or use recreational drugs; and (8) how easy it will be for you to discontinue the medication down the road.

Medications that are useful for treating social anxiety disorder include certain antidepressants, as well as drugs that are traditionally used to treat anxiety. In addition, there is preliminary evidence supporting certain other medications. Each of these approaches is reviewed in the following sections.

Antidepressants

You may be wondering why antidepressants would be recommended for treating problems with anxiety, especially for someone who isn't feeling depressed. In fact, antidepressants are used to treat a wide range of problems, including anxiety disorders, eating disorders, smoking, migraine headaches, and, of course, depression. Just as aspirin can be used both to reduce pain and to prevent heart attacks, antidepressants also have many uses. In the case of social anxiety disorder, antidepressants are the most thoroughly studied medications and are usually considered as the first option. Also, as mentioned earlier, all three of the FDA-approved drugs for social anxiety disorder are antidepressants.

Antidepressants share a number of features. First, they all take several weeks before they begin to have a positive effect on anxiety or depression. Side effects, however, typically begin soon after the medication is started, and they may be worst in the early weeks of treatment. It is generally recommended that people continue taking these medications for a year or more, before trying to reduce the dosage or discontinue taking it.

SELECTIVE SEROTONIN REUPTAKE INHIBITORS (SSRIS)

The SSRIs are a type of antidepressant that affects the levels of *serotonin* (a brain chemical that transmits information from one brain cell to another). They are also the most commonly prescribed medications for social anxiety disorder. The SSRIs include drugs such as paroxetine (Paxil), sertraline (Zoloft), fluoxetine (Prozac), fluvoxamine (Luvox), citalopram (Celexa), and escitalopram (Lexapro). At this time, there is more research that supports the use of paroxetine, sertraline, and fluvoxamine to treat social anxiety disorder than there is for the other SSRIs, but in all probability any of these drugs is likely to be effective because they all have similar effects on the brain.

The side effects of SSRIs vary slightly from drug to drug, but the most common ones include nausea and other abdominal symptoms, sexual dysfunction, dizziness, tremor, rash, insomnia, nervousness, fatigue, dry mouth, sweating, and palpitations. In very rare cases, more serious side effects may occur.

Many of the most common symptoms tend to improve after the first few weeks of treatment, although sexual side effects often continue over time. Recent research suggests that sildenafil citrate (Viagra) can reduce sexual dysfunction in men who are taking SSRIs (Nurnberg et al. 2003). It is generally recommended that SSRIs be started at low dosages and that the dosages should be increased slowly to minimize side effects when treating anxiety.

Most SSRIs can be discontinued fairly easily, but stopping the use of these drugs (or any medication, for that matter) should take place only under the supervision of your doctor. It is not unusual for people to experience withdrawal symptoms while coming off an SSRI, including insomnia, agitation, tremor, anxiety, nausea, diarrhea, dry mouth, weakness, sweating, or abnormal ejaculation. Paroxetine tends to be associated with more withdrawal symptoms than the other SSRIs.

Resuming the medication usually reverses these symptoms within a few hours, and discontinuing the medication very slowly can minimize the symptoms, or completely prevent them from occurring. The table below provides a summary of the SSRIs and the dosages at which they are typically prescribed.

Selective Serotonin Reuptake Inhibitors (SSRIs)

Generic Name	Trade Name	Starting Dose	Daily Dosage
Citalopram*	Celexa	10 mg	10–60 mg
Escitalopram*	Lexapro	10 mg	10–50 mg
Fluoxetine*	Prozac	10–20 mg	10–80 mg
Fluvoxamine	Luvox	50 mg	50–300 mg
Paroxetine*	Paxil	10 mg	10–50 mg
	Paxil CR**	12.5 mg	25–62.5 mg
Sertraline	Zoloft	50 mg	50–200 mg

Notes

*Citalopram, escitalopram, fluoxetine, and paroxetine are also available in liquid form. There is also a new formulation of fluoxetine that can be taken once per week.

**CR = Controlled Release

OTHER ANTIDEPRESSANTS

A number of other antidepressants have been found to be useful for treating social anxiety disorder. Of these, the extended release formula of venlafaxine (Effexor XR) is the only one that has official approval from the FDA, and it is probably the best option, given the available research at this time. Like the SSRIs, venlafaxine acts on serotonin in the brain, but it also acts on another chemical messenger in the brain, *norepinephrine*. Common side effects of venlafaxine include nausea, sexual dysfunction, insomnia, dizziness, tremor, weakness, and dry mouth, and they are generally worse at higher dosages. As with the SSRIs, stopping venlafaxine abruptly can trigger uncomfortable withdrawal symptoms, including insomnia, dizziness, nervousness, dry mouth, headache, weakness, sweating, or sexual dysfunction. Typically, these symptoms last about a week after stopping the medication.

Phenelzine (Nardil) (a type of antidepressant known as a *monoamine oxidase inhibitor* or *MAOI*) has also been shown to be effective for treating social anxiety disorder, but it is rarely used today because of rather extreme side effects, a tendency to interact with other medications, and a number of strict dietary restrictions that must be followed when taking this type of drug.

Moclobemide (Manerix) is related to the MAOIs, but it doesn't have many of the problems that are typically associated with these drugs. The side effects, drug interactions, and dietary restrictions are much more manageable for moclobemide than they are for traditional MAOIs. However, the evidence regarding whether moclobemide is useful for social anxiety disorder has been mixed. Some studies have found it to be useful, whereas others have found no differences in the effectiveness of moclobemide when tested against a *placebo* (an inactive pill that contains no real medication). A review of these studies is available elsewhere (e.g., Antony and McCabe 2003). Note that moclobemide is not available in the United States.

Other antidepressants that have been studied for social anxiety disorder include nefazodone (Serzone) and mirtazapine (Remeron). Initial studies suggest that these drugs may be useful for social anxiety disorder, but there are relatively few studies, and the studies that have been published are based on small numbers of patients and failed to include a placebo comparison group. To evaluate the true effectiveness of a medication, it is essential to compare the medication to a placebo, since many individuals with anxiety problems report an improvement in symptoms following treatment with a placebo. It seems that for many of us, simply *expecting to feel better* is enough to trigger a decrease in anxiety symptoms. Until we have placebo-controlled studies of nefazodone and mirtazapine, it will be difficult to know the extent to which they are useful for treating social anxiety disorder.

The table below provides a summary of antidepressants other than SSRIs that have at least some research supporting their use for social anxiety disorder, as well as the typical dosages at which they are prescribed.

Antidepressants Used to Treat Social Anxiety Disorder Other Than SSRIs

Generic Name	Trade Name	Starting Dose	Daily Dosage
Mirtazapine	Remeron	15 mg	15–60 mg
Moclobemide*	Manerix	150–300 mg	300–600 mg
Nefazodone	Serzone	100–200 mg	100–600 mg
Phenelzine	Nardil	15–30 mg	45–90 mg
Venlafaxine	Effexor XR	37.5–75 mg	75–225 mg

*Moclobemide is not available in the United States.

Other Medication Options

Although antidepressants are perhaps the most popular medications for social anxiety disorder, there are also other drugs effective for treating this condition. The most popular of these are the antianxiety medications, including the benzodiazepines, which are commonly used to treat anxiety and sleep problems. Although there are a number of benzodiazepines that have been shown to be useful for treating anxiety (for example, diazepam or Valium; lorazepam or Ativan), the only two that have been investigated for social anxiety disorder are clonazepam (Klonapin in the United States, and Rivotril in Canada) and alprazolam (Xanax). The typical starting dosage for alprazolam and clonazepam is .5 mg per day, and the maximum daily dose for each is usually in the range of 4 to 6 mg.

The most common side effects for the benzodiazepines include drowsiness, light-headedness, depression, headache, confusion, dizziness, unsteadiness, insomnia, and nervousness.

These drugs should not be taken with alcohol, and they may also affect a person's ability to drive. One big advantage of the medications like alprazolam and clonazepam is that they start working within minutes, unlike the antidepressants, which usually take several weeks to work. A major disadvantage of these drugs is that they can be associated with significant withdrawal symptoms, including feelings of anxiety, arousal, and insomnia. Although these withdrawal symptoms are temporary, they can be quite unpleasant, making it difficult for some people to discontinue these drugs. Therefore, benzodiazepines should be discontinued gradually, and only under the supervision of your doctor.

Another class of drugs sometimes used for treating social anxiety are the beta-adrenergic blockers, which include medications such as propanolol (Inderal). Although these medications are usually used to treat high blood pressure, they also decrease certain physical symptoms of fear, including palpitations and shakiness. They are not particularly useful for treating full-blown social anxiety disorder, but they do seem to help with the mild stage fright often experienced by actors, musicians, and people who have to speak in front of groups. Typically, propanolol is taken in a single dose of 5 to 10 mg, about twenty to thirty minutes before a performance.

Gabapentin (Neurontin) is a medication used to prevent seizures that also appears to reduce anxiety. Preliminary studies in people with social anxiety disorder suggest that gabapentin may be useful. Typically, this medication is started at 300 to 400 mg per day, and is gradually increased to a daily dosage of up to 3600 mg per day.

Finally, herbal products are becoming increasingly popular for treating anxiety, depression, and related problems. Despite their popularity, these remedies should be used with caution. In many cases, we know little about whether herbal remedies work, why they work, whether they have side effects or withdrawal symptoms, or how they interact with other medications. Furthermore, the few products that have been studied for use with depression and anxiety (e.g., inositol, St. John's wort, kava kava, omega-3 fatty acids) have not been studied in people with social anxiety disorder.

In fact, currently there are no published studies of any herbal remedies or other complementary medicine approaches for social anxiety disorder. The best we can say at this time is that there may be herbal treatments that are useful for social anxiety disorder, but until researchers have systematically studied these products for this particular problem, the question of whether herbal remedies are effective for social anxiety remains unanswered.

Stages in Medication Treatment

There are five stages involved in treating anxiety with medications: (1) assessment, (2) initiation, (3) dose escalation, (4) maintenance, and (5) discontinuation.

During the *assessment* phase, your doctor will ask you questions to help determine which medication is best for you. Specifically, your doctor will want to determine the main problem requiring treatment, any other problems that may be present, which medications you have tried in the past, whether you or a family member has previously responded to any particular drugs, and which side effects might be most problematic, given your situation.

During the *initiation* phase, your doctor will likely start the medication at a relatively low dosage, to allow your body time to adjust to the drug. *Dose escalation* is usually gradual. The goal of this stage is to gradually increase the amount of medication being taken until the optimal dosage is reached. This is the dosage that maximizes the benefits of the drug while minimizing the side effects. For some individuals, a particular drug may not be effective, or the side effects may be too intense. In these cases, the medication is gradually discontinued, and a different drug or some alternative treatment may be tried.

Maintenance is the fourth stage in treatment. During this phase, the individual continues to take the drug for an extended period of time. In the case of antidepressants, this stage typically lasts a year or more, in order to minimize the possibility of a return of symptoms when the drug is stopped. For the benzodiazepines, such as alprazolam and clonazepam, it is often recommended that individuals stay on the drug for as brief a time as possible, in order to minimize any difficulty when coming off the medication.

The final stage of treatment is *discontinuation*. At some point during treatment, most individuals eventually will try to decrease the dosage of their medication, or to discontinue the drug completely. Although symptoms often may return during this phase, some people are able to discontinue their medication, or at least to reduce the dosage, without experiencing a return of their social anxiety. If the symptoms do worsen, the medication can be initiated again, usually with the same benefits as before.

In some cases, more than one medication may be used in combination with another drug. For example, some doctors will combine a benzodiazepine with an antidepressant during the early phases of treatment, so the benzodiazepine can begin working on the anxiety right away, while the patient waits for the antidepressant to begin working. A month later, when the antidepressant kicks in, the benzodiazepine can be discontinued slowly.

Combining Medications with Other Approaches

In practice, medications are often combined with other treatment approaches, including cognitive behavioral therapy or another form of psychotherapy. At this time, there is very little research available on combining psychological treatments with medications for social anxiety disorder. However, based on findings from other anxiety disorders, for which the effects of combined treatments are better understood, it is likely that pairing medications and cognitive behavioral therapy may be the best approach for some individuals. Nevertheless, many individuals will probably do just as well with either psychological treatment or medications. In other words, combining two or more approaches to treatment doesn't necessarily lead to a better outcome.

If you begin cognitive behavioral therapy and medication at the same time, you won't be able to pinpoint the treatment component that contributes most to reducing your anxiety. Therefore, in many cases, the best approach is to start with either medication or psychological treatment and see what happens. If you find that your symptoms don't improve, or that they improve only partially despite an adequate course of treatment, you can then consider adding the component of treatment that was missing.

7

Coping with Rejection

Fear of rejection is a trait shared by most of us, and it's probably a good thing, at least in moderation. Avoiding rejection helps us to avoid some of the other negative consequences that can come with having others dislike us. People who have no fear of rejection can sometimes come across as arrogant, which can be offensive to others. Too little fear of rejection also can lead people to avoid striving to succeed, either at their jobs or in their relationships. Often a fear of negative evaluation motivates people to do well. To some extent, the fear of rejection encourages our concern about making a good impression on others.

Given that most of us don't like being rejected, it is unfortunate that rejection is such a normal and frequent occurrence when interacting with other people. Almost everyone has been turned down for a date, ignored by another person, or rejected after applying for a job. Although there are some people who usually seem to have things go their way, that simply isn't the case for most of us.

People who are particularly shy or socially anxious are often much more sensitive to rejection than those people who are less anxious. Therefore, shy or socially anxious people react to rejection (or the threat of rejection) with greater levels of anxiety, depression, or anger. This chapter is all about learning to cope better with the possibility, or the reality, of being rejected.

Note that the strategies described in this chapter build upon those from earlier chapters (especially chapters 3, 4, and 5), so make sure you have read those chapters carefully before turning your attention to this chapter. The ideas discussed in chapter 5 may help to reduce the likelihood of being rejected in social situations, whereas the material in chapters 3 and 4 will reduce the impact of the rejection when it does occur. The purpose of this chapter is to provide additional suggestions for how to deal effectively with rejection.

The Meaning of Rejection

One of the reasons that rejection is so difficult is that people often interpret a rejection as an indication of weakness, failure, or inadequacy. Examples of assumptions that underlie a fear of rejection include:

- If I am rejected by another person, it means that there is something wrong with me.

- If people don't want to spend time with me, that means that they don't like me.

- If someone is bored when I am talking, it means that I am a boring person.

- If I am rejected when I ask this person out, it means that I will probably always be rejected.

- If I am rejected for this job, my friends will think less of me.

In reality, there are many different reasons for rejection. For example, consider the second assumption listed above (if people don't want to spend time with me, that means that they don't like me). In fact, there are many other possible reasons why someone might not want to spend time with you that have nothing to do with whether they like you, or whether you are a likable person in general. Here are some examples:

- Perhaps the other person is too busy to spend time with you (for example, with work, raising young children, dealing with a major life stress).

- Perhaps the person is somewhat introverted, and prefers not to socialize much with anyone other than his or her closest friends.

- Perhaps the person has enough friends, and isn't seeking to expand his or her social network any further.

- Perhaps the other person perceives you to have little in common with him or her (generally, people tend to be more attracted to those who share their interests).

- Perhaps the other person is unaware that you are interested in spending time with him or her.

Note that all of these factors have more to do with the other person than they do with you. Just because one person seems uninterested in socializing with you doesn't mean that other people will necessarily feel the same way.

What if the other person really doesn't like you? Remember, there is a discussion in chapter 3 of the fact that it is impossible for everyone to like you. The very things that make you attractive or interesting to one person will necessarily make you less attractive and less interesting to another person, because we all find different qualities interesting and attractive. It hurts when we are attracted to another person (for example, as a potential friend), and that person doesn't share our interest or attraction. But why should we expect any one person to want to spend time with us? The key is to remember that even if you are rejected in a particular situation, or by a particular person, the experience tells you little about whether you will be rejected in a different situation, or by a different person. It also says little about you, and whether you are likable, interesting, or attractive. Even the most personable individuals among us experience rejection from time to time.

Exercise: Why Did You Feel Rejected?

Think back to the last time you experienced rejection from another person. This may include another person turning down your invitation to socialize, making a negative comment, or staring at you with a bored look. On a fresh page in your journal, record your negative interpretation that led you to feel rejected. Next, record as many alternative explanations as possible for why the rejection may have occurred. How might someone else who tolerated rejection well have interpreted the experience if it had happened to him or her?

Remove the Pressure

When the perceived cost of rejection is very high, people tend to invest too much energy in the outcome of each and every social interaction where rejection may be a possible outcome. For example, a person who fears being turned down when applying for a job may have taken months to work up the courage to apply for that job. That person will often feel very anxious while waiting to find out whether he or she will be granted an interview, and may feel devastated if things don't work out.

Unfortunately, assigning that much importance to the outcome of a specific social interaction or situation usually leads to failure and disappointment. In fact, others may even sense your desperation, which can increase the likelihood of rejection (nobody likes to feel pressured into hiring someone for a job, going on a date, or spending time with another person).

Instead, it is preferable to focus on the process rather than the outcome of our social interactions. Make the most of social opportunities, but be prepared for things not to work out the way you want them to. When you allow yourself to take risks in social situations (for example, asking a coworker to have lunch, trying to make small talk at a party, or asking someone out on a date), expect that your efforts will sometimes lead to rejection, and be ready to move on when things don't work out as planned. If you are rejected, you can still learn something from the experience. For example, you may learn what *not* to do next time you are in a similar situation.

Take More Risks

The more social risks you take, the more rejections you will experience. In fact, it is the possibility of rejection that probably stops you from taking more social risks than you do. For example, if you tend to avoid dating, asking friends to get together, applying for jobs, or simply asking a stranger for directions, it may be for fear that the other people involved will think badly of you.

You may believe that you need to protect yourself from rejection by avoiding it at all costs. In fact, the opposite is more likely to be true. It may actually be important to *inoculate* yourself against the effects of rejection by allowing yourself to be rejected from time to time. When people are inoculated against developing a particular disease, they are given a small amount of the germ that causes the disease, which allows the body to produce the antibodies needed to fight the disease in the event that the germs are later encountered in full force. In a similar way, exposure to normal levels of rejection, in a planned and controlled way, may help you to deal better with the effects of being rejected when it happens in the future.

Rejection is one of the natural consequences of interacting with others. As reviewed earlier, increasing the frequency with which you take social risks will lead to more frequent rejections. However, taking more risks in social situations will also lead to more frequent successes.

Let's assume, for the sake of argument, that the statistical likelihood of someone accepting your invitation for a date is one in three, and that the likelihood of a particular date leading to a second date is also one in three. If you never ask anyone out, you might never have the opportunity to date. If you ask someone out once each year, every three years you will have the opportunity to go on a date, and every nine years you will get to go out with the same person more than once. However, if you ask a different person to go out with you every day, chances are that someone will accept your offer every three days, and every nine days you will date a person who is interested in going out for a second date. Before long, you will be dating more people than you know what to do with. The point is this: by risking the possibility of rejection, you will experience more frequent successes as well as more frequent rejections.

There are a number of ways to prepare for rejections that may occur as a result of taking more risks. First, simply expect that sometimes people will reject you. That way rejection won't be a surprise when it happens, and it should be easier to cope with it. Second, review in advance all the different reasons why you might be rejected (including positive, neutral, and negative explanations), so you don't walk into the situation focusing only on the most negative interpretations. Finally, ask yourself the question, "So what if I am rejected?" Rather than emphasizing how terrible that would be, try to focus on how you can cope with the situation, how you can get past it, and what you can do differently, if anything, to avoid being rejected next time.

Exercise: Take Some Risks

In the next week, plan to take a social risk. It may include applying for a job, inviting people to a party, asking a coworker to join you for lunch, submitting an article to a magazine for possible publication, taking an art class with other people, or any other situation where you fear being judged by others. On a fresh page in your journal, record the possible outcomes of confronting the situation, and brainstorm the ways in which you will be able to cope with each potential outcome.

Are You Contributing to Your Own Rejection?

So far, this chapter has emphasized the idea that if you persevere, take frequent social risks, and learn to stop the cycle of catastrophic thinking that often occurs after being rejected, dealing with rejection will become less of a problem for you. In many cases, that is true. However, in addition to changing your reaction to rejection, there may also be things you can do to reduce the likelihood of being rejected. For example, chapter 5 discussed strategies for improving communication, which may help to improve how others view your behavior in social situations.

If you find that you are being rejected over and over, it may be useful to ask yourself why that is happening. Frequent rejection may simply be bad luck, but it may also reflect some persistent issue that is contributing to the problem, and that will likely continue to cause rejection in the future.

If there is a reason for the repeated rejection, your first step would be to consider whether it is related to something you are doing, or something about the situation in which the rejection occurs. Some examples of behaviors that can sometimes lead to a negative impression on others include

- Extremes in personality, such as a tendency to come across as overly rigid, laid-back, outgoing, introverted, dependent, aloof, depressed, anxious, irritable, and so on.

- Extremes in appearance, such as dressing too formally or informally for the situation

- Anxious behaviors, such as poor eye contact, standing far away, talking too quietly, fidgeting, avoidance

- Extreme communication styles such as talking too much (e.g., giving too many details), talking too little, arguing, coming across as condescending

It may be that changing some of these or other problem behaviors will lead to greater success in social situations.

Alternatively, repeated rejection can be related to factors that have more to do with the situation than with the person who's been rejected. For example, in a recession, many people have trouble finding work. After the technology crash of 2000, tens of thousands of people working in the technology sector lost their jobs and most had difficulty finding new jobs in their areas of expertise. Unfortunately, there is not much you can do to avoid rejection when it is related to factors over which you have little control.

Finally, repeated rejection may be a result of an interaction between a person's behavior and a person's environment. Specifically, some individuals tend to seek out social interactions that are likely to end in rejection. Examples may include dating others who are very critical, applying for jobs for which one is unqualified, or seeking friendship with someone who is not interested in making new friends. For a social relationship to work, there has to be a good match between all those involved. When you seek approval from someone who is unable or unwilling to provide it, most likely it will end with you feeling rejected.

On the other hand, approval is often quite easy to get under the right circumstances, so being selective about the people from whom you wish to receive approval and acceptance will be helpful.

8

Meet New People

By this point, you've read about how to change your anxious thoughts, how to confront the situations you fear, and how to improve your communication skills. You've also learned about medications that can be useful for reducing anxiety symptoms in people with social anxiety disorder. One problem that hasn't been discussed thus far, however, is the issue of how to go about enlarging your social network. People who are very shy or who experience high levels of anxiety in social situations often find it difficult to begin new relationships and to make new friends. The purpose of this chapter is to discuss ideas for how and where to meet new people.

Where Most People Meet

In 1994, Laumann et al. published the results of a survey of more than three thousand Americans that included questions about the ways and places in which people met one another.

The survey focused on the ways in which couples meet, but the results may be just as relevant for people who are interested in developing other types of relationships, including making new friends, and even making the social connections needed to find a new job.

Among the married couples in the survey, the most frequent way in which people met their spouses was through an introduction by a friend (35 percent of those surveyed met their spouse in this way). The second most common way of meeting one's spouse was by introducing oneself (32 percent). Other common ways of meeting included an introduction by a family member (15 percent), or by a coworker (6 percent), or a classmate (6 percent).

The survey also asked about the locations in which people meet their spouses. Thirty-eight percent of respondents reported having met their spouse at work or at school. Other common meeting places includes parties (10 percent), a place of worship such as a church (8 percent), a bar (8 percent), and a gym or social club (4 percent). When this survey was published (before most of us had even heard of the Internet), fewer than 1 percent of people reported having met their spouses through personal ads. However, in the last decade, Internet dating has become very popular. If this survey were to be conducted today, one might expect "the Internet" to appear as another popular way of meeting potential partners. This chapter will return to the topic of meeting people on the Internet later.

For unmarried couples (including couples living together, couples in long-term relationships, and couples who had only recently started dating), the ways and locations in which people met were similar to those for the married couples (Laumann et al. 1994). However, there were a few minor differences. For example, couples who had just started dating were more likely than married couples to have met in a bar or at a party, whereas long-term relationships were more likely to have begun in another way.

Where to Meet New People

Meeting new people requires making yourself available to opportunities as they arise, but also creating opportunities that may not come up naturally in your life. Social situations with repeated contact (for example, at work) are more likely to lead to the development of a friendship or relationship than are situations where you just meet someone once (for example, going to a bar). Of course, social anxiety can make it difficult for some people to take advantage of social opportunities when they arise. Therefore, it is important that you continue to use the techniques discussed throughout this book, including the strategies for dealing with possible rejection (see chapter 7), as you make an effort to meet new people. Examples of places where you may meet new people easily are discussed throughout the remainder of this section.

WORK

Almost one in six married people met his or her spouse in the workplace (Laumann et al. 1994). Many more people develop close friendships with people at work. Relationships with coworkers may begin casually, perhaps by saying hello at the photocopy machine. Before long, coworkers start to share more about their personal lives (for example, news about their families or what they did on the weekend), and they begin to discover that they have interests or experiences in common. They may decide to have lunch together, or to spend time together outside of working hours. Over time, a friendship may develop.

VOLUNTEERING

Volunteer work can provide many of the same social advantages as a more traditional work setting. Opportunities for volunteering are about as varied as opportunities for other

types of work. Volunteers work in schools, hospitals, and char-
itable organizations. There are also numerous volunteers working in creative fields, such as theater and visual arts (for
example, ushering at performances, painting sets, sewing cos-
tumes, helping to organize art exhibitions, etc.). If you are part
of a professional association, volunteering to sit on a commit-
tee or to help out with some project will also provide you with
opportunities to meet new people. For suggestions on volunteer opportunities in your area, check out the Web site
www.volunteermatch.org.

SCHOOL

For full-time students, meeting people at school may be
the most common way to develop relationships and make
friends. Even if you are not a full-time student, taking a course
in an area that interests you is an ideal way to expand your
social network. Like work, school offers an opportunity to
have repeated contact with the same people over time. Also, if
the course you take is in a topic that interests you (e.g., a
cooking class, art class, university course on world religions, or
an aerobics class), the chances are good that you will meet
other people who share your interests. Of course, it's possible
to take an entire course and meet no one. In order to actually
develop relationships, it will be important to use the skills that
you've learned and practiced throughout this book, and to
take social risks when you are at school.

HOBBIES

People who have hobbies often enjoy meeting others who
share similar interests. Joining a club or organization that
focuses on your hobby can be a fantastic way to meet people
who are interested in the same things that you are. How can
you find out about such clubs? A good place to start is the
Internet (for example, start a search on www.google.com). For

instance, if you love hiking and you live in Chicago, try searching for the terms "hiking club Chicago." Dozens of options will come up (some more useful than others). You may be surprised how many clubs and organizations there are for just about every hobby or interest, including reading, photography, collecting, crafts, travel, sports, pets, and so on. If you would like to meet people who share your interests, but the option of joining a club does not appeal to you, there are often other options. For example, if you are interested in travel, taking a trip and staying in a hostel will provide you with many opportunities to meet other people who also enjoy traveling.

SPORTS AND EXERCISE

If you enjoy engaging in sports, fitness activities, and exercise, the best way to meet other people who share your interests is to make a point of being in places where people who like athletics tend to go. Joining a gym or a sports team or taking a fitness class are obvious choices. If you decide to join a gym, attending on the same days each week, and at the same time each day will increase the likelihood of seeing the same people time and time again. With repeated contact, it may be easier to strike up a conversation, schedule a basketball or tennis game together, or break for a cold drink after an aerobics class.

SOCIAL EVENTS

Attending social gatherings is another obvious way to meet people, and to enrich relationships with people whom you already know. For example, attending a party with your coworkers allows you to get to know them in a very different context than work. In fact, offering to host a party for your colleagues in your own home is a great way to allow your colleagues the opportunity to get to know you better. In addition to parties with coworkers, making a point of attending other social gatherings, especially with people who share your interests, will open up opportunities for getting to know new people. For example, openings of shows at a local art gallery, high school reunions, and singles dances all provide possibilities for making new social contacts and enriching old contacts.

DATING SERVICES, PERSONAL ADS, AND THE INTERNET

Increasingly, peoples' busy schedules are forcing them to seek new ways to meet other people for dating and possibly for developing long-term relationships. Dating services, Internet chat rooms, and personal ads are just a few examples. Dating services vary in quality, cost, and the types of services they offer. Some services cater more to particular types of people (for example, professionals), and some use quite sophisticated ways of matching people up, including psychological testing. If you decide to try a dating service, it would probably be a good idea to shop around for a service that is right for your needs.

Some people have had great success with personal ads, including those that appear in newspapers, telephone personal ad services, and on the Internet (for example, Internet dating services such as match.com). Nevertheless, if you choose to meet people through personal ads, be sure to be cautious. Get to know the person first over the phone, and be sure to meet in a public place the first time. Initially, arrange just a short meeting (perhaps for coffee or tea) so if things don't work out, you can end the relationship immediately. Keep your expectations realistic. Meetings through personal ads, dating services, and blind dates often do not amount to much more than a casual acquaintance, though some great relationships have begun this way. If nothing else, dating through personal ads will provide you with opportunities to practice the other strategies described in this book.

The Internet is increasingly becoming a popular way to meet new people. For example, one study found that more than 60 percent of unmarried university students had been successful in developing an online friendship (Knox et al. 2001). In fact, about half of these individuals reported that they felt more comfortable meeting people online than in person. Another survey (Nice and Katzev 1998) also found that the Internet has become a common way to make friends and develop romantic relationships. Furthermore, among those surveyed, the quality of the online relationships (for example, the degree of closeness, satisfaction, and communication) was as strong as the quality of the respondents' off-line relationships.

Up to a third of those who use the Internet regularly to meet people eventually wind up meeting their cyberfriends in person (McCown et al. 2001). But beware: 40 percent of respondents in one survey reported that they lied about themselves during the course of meeting new people online (Knox et al. 2001). Not surprisingly, a tendency to misrepresent features such as age and physical appearance are more common in online relationships than in real-life relationships (Cornwall and Lundgren 2001).

There is one other warning to heed: Internet relationships should not be thought of as a replacement for relationships in other parts of your life. To overcome problems with social anxiety and shyness, it will be important to confront the situations you fear, and to improve the quality of your relationships, even when you are away from your computer.

Meeting the Right Types of People

A first step for meeting a new friend or for developing a new relationship is to have some idea of what you are looking for. No one person can fulfill all, or even most, of your social needs. Different relationships have different functions. It is not unusual for people to have some relationships that are based on a particular activity (e.g., a friend to go jogging with), and other relationships that fulfill other roles and functions. Different relationships can give you companionship, provide emotional support, or simply help you to pass the time in a pleasant way.

What types of friendships or relationships are you seeking? If you are looking for a friend to join you for a movie every couple of weeks, you probably will want to look for a different type of person than if you are looking for a partner with whom you can settle down and raise children. If your goal is to add some excitement to your life, seeking someone who is adventurous, gorgeous, passionate, and spontaneous may be for you.

On the other hand, these exciting qualities may become less important once the initial thrill of a new relationship dies down. In a more mature relationship, qualities such as honesty, shared values, respect, and stability may be more important. Knowing what you want from a friendship or relationship can help you decide with whom to invest your time.

In reality, however, it is often difficult to know what qualities are important to you until you are actually in a friendship or relationship. You may have always believed that you could be friends only with someone who shares your political views, and later you may have discovered that a shared political ideology is less important to you than you once thought. Still, if you are seeking a particular type of person for friendship, make sure you participate in activities that will increase your chances of meeting such a person. This may sound obvious, but sometimes it's important to state the obvious. That is, if you want to meet a man, don't hang around places where there are mostly women present. If you don't enjoy drinking, don't try to meet people in bars.

Exercise: Meet One New Person

Over the next few weeks, make a plan to meet at least one new person. This could happen by talking to someone new at work or school, signing up to take a class, starting a new volunteer position, or any other method that occurs to you. Record your progress in your journal. If your first attempt doesn't work out, keep trying until you are able to form a new friendship or relationship. Record all of your efforts in your journal.

9

Learn to Make Presentations with Confidence

As stated in chapter 1, the fear of performing is one of the most common types of social anxiety. Performance situations that are often feared include obvious ones like public speaking, acting, and singing in front of others, but they may also include more subtle performance situations, such as eating or drinking in front of others, making mistakes in public, writing in front of others, or even being stared at while walking down the street. This chapter begins with a brief review of strategies for becoming more comfortable in performance situations, especially when giving presentations. Then, pointers are provided on how to improve the quality of your presentations.

Dealing with the Fear of Performing

If you've read the previous chapters, you probably have a good idea of how to overcome the fears of performing and of being the center of attention. Identifying and changing your anxious thoughts, along with frequent exposure to the situations you fear, will probably lead to dramatic improvements in your performance anxiety. Also, as reviewed in chapter 6, certain medications to reduce the fear and anxiety associated with performance situations have proven effective.

Concerns about performing and public speaking usually center around fears of appearing foolish, unattractive, boring, overly anxious, or incompetent. People who avoid being the center of attention often assume that allowing themselves to be observed by others can lead only to horrible consequences. In reality, over time, the costs of avoiding these feared situations are often greater than the risks of confronting them directly. Chapter 3 provides detailed instructions for conquering the negative thinking that typically leads to anxiety in performance situations. Essentially, the goals of cognitive therapy are to learn to think more realistically, to recognize that the chances of looking foolish are probably much lower than you imagine, and to learn to tolerate the possibility that matters may not go as well as you hope they will.

Every day, people across the world give mediocre presentations, make mistakes, dress badly, have boring conversations, and show visible signs of anxiety without having to suffer terrible consequences. As awful as it feels to be anxious in front of others, from time to time you can afford to come across poorly. Even if your audience dislikes your presentation, or if you miss out on making a sale or landing a new job, there will be other opportunities. In fact, the belief that you must perform perfectly is partly responsible for the anxiety that you experience. If you cared less about how others view your performance, chances are that your performance would improve.

The most direct route to becoming more comfortable when you are the center of attention is to practice being the center of attention until it doesn't bother you anymore. As discussed in chapter 4, exposure to feared situations will lead to a reduction in fear, especially if the exposure is prolonged repeated frequently, and under your control. By allowing yourself to be exposed in performance situations, and by tolerating the discomfort and the possibility of performing poorly, your self-confidence will improve.

In addition to dealing with your fear, there are a number of strategies you can use to make the most of your presentations. The remainder of this chapter discusses methods of improving the quality of your presentations.

Improving Your Presentations

Whether you need to make a brief toast at a party or teach a daylong workshop to your colleagues at work, there are a number of strategies to keep in mind to ensure that your presentation will be effective. This section provides a few ideas to improve the quality of your presentations. For a more detailed discussion of this topic, a number of excellent books are available online and in bookstores (Bowman 1998; Buchan 1997; Davidson 2003; Kushner 1996).

PREPARING FOR PRESENTATIONS

If you know in advance that you will be giving a presentation, there are a number of steps you can take to prepare. These involve (1) understanding the purpose of your presentation, (2) knowing your audience, (3) organizing your presentation, and (4) rehearsing your presentation. Each of these four steps is discussed below.

UNDERSTAND THE PURPOSE OF YOUR PRESENTATION. Is the ʋrpose of the presentation to *entertain* your audience? To ʋnce your audience of something (for example, to buy a ⁺o accept a new idea)? Is it to *teach* a new skill? ʋn the purpose of your presentation, the content of ʋn should be very different. For example, if the ʋresentation is to entertain, you may include

ʋe Solutions to Shyness

more jokes or perhaps add music to your talk. On the other hand, if the purpose is to teach a new skill, it may be important to include detailed handouts or to provide audience members with opportunities to practice their new skills (for example, distribute practical exercises for them to try out the new skill you are teaching).

KNOW YOUR AUDIENCE. It is useful to know the size of your audience and their composition with respect to age, gender, and professional background. You will also want to understand what the audience may be expecting from you, what they already know, and what they need to find out during your presentation. Remember, your presentation should be designed with your audience in mind. If you are to give a speech at your best friend's wedding, it may be received poorly if it is filled with insider jokes that only you and the bride or groom will understand.

Similarly, if you are to give a lecture to a group of professionals, it is important not to pitch the lecture at a level that is either too complex or too simplistic. If you are unsure of your audience's composition, sometimes it can be useful to ask them a few relevant questions about their backgrounds or their level of familiarity with the topic before beginning your presentation.

ORGANIZE YOUR PRESENTATION. When preparing your presentation, think of the material in terms of three main sections: the introduction, the main body of the presentation, and the conclusion. The introduction should orient your audience to the material and provide an overview of what you intend to cover. The main body of the talk should include the primary information that you are presenting. The conclusion should provide closure by summarizing the main points of the presentation and discussing some of the implications or interpretations of those key points, so your audience will understand why your presentation was important.

REHEARSE THE PRESENTATION. If you are not accustomed to giving presentations, or if you are not familiar with the material you are presenting, rehearsing your talk in front of colleagues, friends, family members, or even a mirror can be useful. Rehearsing the talk will also help to reduce your level of anxiety. If you have a video camera, you might consider videotaping your rehearsed presentation and then watching it to see if there is anything you should change.

SPEAKING EFFECTIVELY

Suggestions for avoiding some of the most common mistakes made by presenters are provided below. If you follow these simple guidelines, that should greatly improve the quality of your presentations.

- Speak clearly, and at a volume that can be heard at the back of the room.

- Be sure not to mispronounce any words. Check the pronunciation of any words you are not sure about.

- Avoid saying "um," "uh," or "er," as much as you can.

- Make eye contact with people in your audience.

- Move around when you are speaking, and gesture with your hands. Don't keep your hands in your pockets or cross your arms.

- Don't talk too quickly or try to squeeze too much information into the talk.

- Audience members will likely miss parts of your presentation as their attention shifts. Repeat your most important points frequently, so your audience can keep track of what you are saying.

- Be yourself. Don't try too hard to appear supersmart or overly entertaining. If the audience perceives you as insincere, your ability to communicate your message will be compromised.

- Be prepared to answer questions as best as you can. At a large presentation, be sure to repeat all questions so those in the back of the room can hear them. If you don't know the answer to a question, just say so. Don't make something up.

ENGAGING YOUR AUDIENCE

Unless you can keep your audience interested in your presentation, your message will not be received. There are a number of tricks that presenters use to bring their talks to life. Some of the most commonly used strategies are listed below.

HUMOR. A relevant cartoon or joke can be a very effective way to hold your audience's attention. However, when not used well, humor can detract from the presentation. Remember that humor is very subjective. A joke that is funny to one person may seem silly or even offensive to another. Try testing your jokes or cartoons on a few trusted people before using them with a larger audience. Also, avoid jokes that are made at another person's expense. If you want to make fun of someone, make fun of yourself. Chances are that if you target some other individual or group, some people in the audience won't be amused.

PERSONAL STORIES OR VIGNETTES. Personal stories also can be a useful way to engage your audience. Make sure that your stories are relevant, and that they don't detract from your credibility, or from the message you are trying to get across.

ILLUSTRATIONS AND EXAMPLES. If you are discussing a complex topic, be sure to use examples and illustrations to help bring your message to life. For example, if you are speaking at your best friend's wedding, give a few examples of the wonderful things he or she has done over the years, rather than simply saying that he or she is a wonderful person. Relevant statistics also can be used to illustrate key points in your presentation, depending on the topic.

SPEAK FOR THE RIGHT LENGTH OF TIME. Don't go on and on about a particular topic any longer than you have to. It can be tempting to say everything you can think of, perhaps to show your audience how smart you are. Try to resist that temptation. Be succinct and to the point.

DON'T READ YOUR PRESENTATION. Often it's best to allow for some spontaneity and improvisation during your presentation. Talks that are memorized or read tend to be less interesting, even monotonous, especially if it's obvious to the audience that it's being read word for word. If possible, try to use an outline detailed enough that you don't omit any key points, but that still allows you to present the information in a fresh and interesting way. Of course, for some presenters (those who have difficulty thinking on their feet), and some topics (particularly complex topics), there may be no option but to read at least parts of the presentation. If that is the case, then make an effort to look at the audience every few sentences instead of keeping your eyes glued to the page you are reading.

ENCOURAGE AUDIENCE PARTICIPATION. Depending on the type of presentation you are giving, it may be helpful to find ways to add some audience participation. Examples would include answering questions from the audience, asking questions of the audience, having an audience member participate in a role-playing demonstration or some other exercise, or testing the audience on the material presented.

AUDIOVISUAL AIDS. Audiovisual aids are frequently used to make presentations more engaging. These may be offered as slides, computer-generated presentations, overhead transparencies, flip charts, handouts, recorded music or messages, videotapes, or CD-ROMs. These supporting materials may include your key points, topic headings, photos, relevant quotes, cartoons, illustrations, or other graphics. You may even decide to include props. For example, if you are discussing a new brochure that you've developed, have copies of it available for people to examine. Make sure your supporting materials enhance your presentation. If your audiovisual aids are too hard to see, too distracting, or too irrelevant, they will detract from your message.

Exercise: Give a New Presentation—Compare It with a Previous One

The next time you have to give a presentation, make an effort to include some of the suggestions described in this chapter. Record in your journal any differences you observe between your newly modified presentation and any presentations you have given in the past. Which strategies were particularly useful? Which will you employ again?

10 Stop Trying to Be Perfect

From the time we are born, other people continually evaluate our behavior, correct our mistakes, and encourage us to improve our performance. For example, parents teach their children to walk, talk, be polite, and clean their rooms. Teachers train their students to read, write, and do arithmetic, and they frequently test their students' skills and provide feedback. From time to time, even our employers, spouses, children, friends, and perfect strangers find it important to evaluate our behavior and correct our mistakes. No wonder some people become overly concerned about doing a perfect job and making a good impression on others.

Setting high standards and striving to achieve them is considered by most people a sign of strength of character. High standards allow some people to reach peak levels of performance in sports, business, academia, and almost every other field. Perfectionism, on the other hand, involves a tendency to set standards that are so high they cannot possibly be met. The standards that perfectionists hold also tend to be inflexible;

and when they are not achieved, the people who hold them may feel depressed, disappointed, anxious, or angry.

With perfectionism, high standards often interfere with performance by causing the perfectionist to procrastinate, avoid situations when there is a risk of making mistakes, or spend huge amounts of time trying to get things right. People who score high in perfectionism tend to hold unrealistic high personal standards, doubt their accomplishments, and worry about making mistakes. They also may hold excessively high standards for others, leading to frustration when their expectations are not met.

This chapter reviews the nature of perfectionism, the relationship between perfectionism and social anxiety, and methods for overcoming perfectionism. If you tend to set unrealistic standards for yourself, and your perfectionism gets in your way, you may benefit from further reading on this topic, including an earlier book, *When Perfect Isn't Good Enough* (Antony and Swinson 1998).

Perfectionism and Social Anxiety

As stated in earlier chapters, a hallmark feature of social anxiety and shyness is the fear of being negatively evaluated by others. Not surprisingly, people with high levels of social anxiety also tend to have higher than normal levels of perfectionism (Antony et al. 1998). In fact, their standards are often much higher for themselves than they are for other people, although some people with high social anxiety also hold high standards for others. Excessive social anxiety is often associated with beliefs such as the following:

- I should be liked by everyone.

- I should always make a good impression on others.

- I should never show signs of anxiety.

- I should always appear to be brilliant, attractive, and interesting.

- I must always do a perfect job at work.

- If I don't come across extremely well, then I have failed.

- Anything less than an "A" on an exam is unacceptable.

Statements that include words like "must," "should," "always," and "never" are often signs of all-or-nothing thinking (see chapter 3). Frequent all-or-nothing thinking can be a sign of perfectionism.

Changing Perfectionistic Thinking

The strategies for changing perfectionistic thinking are similar to those used for changing other types of anxious thinking. First, it is useful to *examine the evidence* for your thoughts, rather than simply accepting them as true. For example, if you assume that it's essential that you always make a good impression when talking to others, ask yourself, "Have I ever said something stupid in front of other people?" If the answer is yes (which is probably the case, if you are like most people), what were the consequences? Perhaps you were teased for a minute or two, or maybe someone gave you a strange look. Or, perhaps no one noticed. Were there any serious or long-term consequences? If not, what does that tell you about whether it is in fact essential that you avoid saying something stupid on front of others? Is it worth all the effort you make to avoid looking foolish?

Another technique that is particularly useful for combating perfectionistic thinking is *perspective taking*. Essentially, this involves trying to see things from another person's point of view. For example, if you are concerned about others finding your new outfit unattractive, you might ask yourself,

"How might someone who is less concerned about looking perfect think about this situation?" Even the most fashionable of dressers occasionally get it wrong, and you can afford not to look your best from time to time. In all likelihood, people will like what you are wearing, and if they don't, you will survive.

Another tool used to combat all-or-nothing thinking involves *compromising*. If the thought of lowering your standards too much is frightening, perhaps it would be okay to lower your standards a bit. If striving to always be the most productive worker in your department leads to problems with your marriage, perhaps you can settle for being one of the top five workers, and allow yourself to spend more time with your spouse. Instead of viewing matters as black and white, compromising involves seeing shades of gray and understanding that situations are often more complex than they seem. In other words, there is often more than one right way to handle a situation.

The tendency to compare oneself to others who are much more confident, accomplished, or skilled is another feature of social anxiety (Antony et al. in press). Not surprisingly, the tendency to feel sad and anxious is a natural consequence of comparing yourself to others who are much better than you are in a particular dimension. It's normal to compare oneself to others—this is one way to determine how your own performance measures up. However, it makes the most sense to compare yourself to others who are at similar levels as yourself (that's what most people do). If you are an amateur painter and you constantly compare your work to that of professionals who exhibit their work in museums, you will just end up feeling bad about yourself. Instead, compare your work to that of other amateur painters.

Finally, try to *look at the big picture*, instead of getting bogged down in the details. For example, if you make a mistake during a presentation, don't focus exclusively on your mistake. Ask yourself, "How was the rest of my presentation?

Will my mistake matter so much tomorrow, next week, or next year?"

Exercise: Record and Challenge Your Perfectionistic Thoughts

Over the next few weeks, record in your journal any perfectionistic thoughts that you notice going through your mind. Under each thought you write down, record any alternative ways of thinking about the situation using the strategies described in the preceding section. In other words, challenge your perfectionistic thoughts instead of assuming they are established facts.

Changing Perfectionistic Behavior

Perfectionistic behaviors can be divided into two main types: behaviors designed to help an individual meet his or her excessively high standards, and avoidance of situations that might require a person to live up to his or her high standards. Examples of the first type of behavior include excessive preparation or rehearsal, and excessive checking or reassurance seeking. Examples of the second type of behavior include avoiding social situations, procrastinating, or finding subtle ways to reduce anxiety, such as drinking alcohol before going to a party.

Although these behaviors are intended to give the person a sense of control in the situation, over the long term, they have precisely the opposite effect, particularly if they are used too frequently. In addition to maintaining anxiety over time, these behaviors often interfere with work, relationships, and other activities. For example, a person who spends days rehearsing a brief presentation will have less time to get other things done, compared to someone who spends only an hour or two on preparation.

EXPOSURE

Chapter 4 provides detailed instructions for using exposure to feared situations to combat social anxiety. Exposure can also be used to decrease perfectionism. For individuals who are fearful of making mistakes or coming across as less than perfect, exposure practices typically involve doing just that—purposely making mistakes and coming across as less than perfect. Furthermore, practicing being in situations where there is a high likelihood that things won't work out perfectly can be useful (provided the situation is one where the consequences of not performing well are manageable). Some examples of relevant exposure exercises include

- Showing up for an appointment on the wrong day.

- Forgetting your ticket when you pick up your dry cleaning.

- Mispronouncing a couple of words during a conversation.

- Having lunch with a friend, and purposely allow several uncomfortable silences to occur.

- Wearing clothes to the mall that you think are unattractive.

- Losing your train of thought during a presentation.

- Sending a letter that includes a few typos.

PREVENTING PROBLEM BEHAVIORS

Another strategy for changing perfectionism is to stop yourself from engaging in excessive behaviors designed to prevent the negative consequences you fear. For example, if you tend to seek reassurance from others on a regular basis, you might try to prevent yourself from doing that. Other examples of this technique include preventing yourself from excessive checking, and stopping yourself from spending too much time preparing for presentations and other social situations. Behaviors expressly designed to prevent you from feeling uncomfortable (for example, drinking alcohol to stay calm at a party, avoiding brightly lit restaurants so no one will notice your blushing) should also be stopped or modified.

Exercise: Practice Being Imperfect

If you have some perfectionistic behaviors that you tend to use a lot (such as taking great pains to avoid looking bad), try doing the opposite. As long as the actual consequences are likely to be mild, purposely try to make a mistake or purposely do something to look foolish. Then, in your journal, record what you did and what the outcome was. What did you learn from the exercise?

Afterword: Planning for the Future

Over a period of a few months, using the strategies described in this book should lead to significant reductions in your social and performance anxiety. Be sure to monitor your progress from time to time by returning to the treatment goals you set in chapter 2. How close are you to reaching your goals? What strategies have been most useful? Are there certain strategies that haven't helped? If so, why not? Is it possible that the strategies have not been used in the most effective way?

If your shyness has improved as a result of using the techniques in this book, your challenge will be to maintain the gains you've made. If you are taking medication (especially antidepressants), be sure to stay on your medication for at least six months to a year in order to minimize the chances of relapse when you try to decrease the dosage or discontinue the medication altogether. Also, make sure that any attempts to decrease your dosage of medication are discussed with your prescribing doctor.

Regular use of the cognitive and behavioral strategies will also help to keep your anxiety at bay. For example, continue to challenge your anxious thoughts when they arise, and be sure to engage in small exposure practices when opportunities arise. If you don't have an exposure for a long period of time (for example, if you have no scheduled presentations for many months), don't be surprised if some of your anxiety returns the next time you encounter the feared situation. The key is to make sure that you don't fall into some of your old ways of coping with the anxiety. Remember that anxiety should be taken as a signal to confront a feared situation, not as a signal to avoid it.

If you have not found the strategies described in this book to be useful, don't give up. Some people need a more structured approach to treatment, and it may be worth considering seeking professional help. If you are interested in finding a clinician in your area, a good place to start is to contact the Anxiety Disorders Association of America (www.adaa.org) or the Anxiety Disorders Association of Canada (www.anxiety canada.ca). These organizations can recommend professionals who specialize in the assessment and treatment of anxiety disorders using cognitive behavior therapy, medication, or both approaches. Finally, additional reading may be useful. Throughout this book, a number of readings have been suggested on various topics related to shyness, perfectionism, and social skills. The list of recommended books at the back of this book includes some additional references that may be useful.

Recommended Readings

Books for Consumers

Antony, M. M., and R. P. Swinson. 2000. *The Shyness and Social Anxiety Workbook: Proven, Step-by-Step Techniques for Overcoming Your Fear*. Oakland, CA: New Harbinger Publications.

Butler, G. 1999. *Overcoming Social Anxiety and Shyness: A Self-Help Guide Using Cognitive Behavioral Techniques*. London: Robinson.

Markway, B. G., C. N. Carmin, C. A. Pollard, and T. Flynn. 1992. *Dying of Embarrassment: Help for Social Anxiety and Phobia*. Oakland, CA: New Harbinger Publications.

Rapee, R. M. 1998. *Overcoming Shyness and Social Phobia: A Step-by-Step Guide*. Northvale, NJ: Jason Aronson.

Schneier, F., and L. Welkowitz. 1996. *The Hidden Face of Shyness: Understanding and Overcoming Social Anxiety*. New York: Avon Books.

Stein, M. B., and J. R. Walker. 2001. *Triumph over Shyness: Conquering Shyness and Social Anxiety*. New York: McGraw Hill.

Books for Professionals

Antony, M. M., and R. P. Swinson. 2000. *Phobic Disorders and Panic in Adults: A Guide to Assessment and Treatment.* Washington, DC: American Psychological Association.

Beidel, D. C., and S. M. Turner. 1998. *Shy Children, Phobic Adults: Nature and Treatment of Social Phobia.* Washington, DC: American Psychological Association.

Crozier, W. R., and L. E. Alden. 2001. *International Handbook of Social Anxiety: Concepts, Research and Interventions Relating to the Self and Shyness.* New York: John Wiley and Sons.

Heimberg, R. G., and R. E. Becker. 2002. *Cognitive-Behavioral Group Therapy for Social Phobia: Basic Mechanisms and Clinical Strategies.* New York: Guilford.

Heimberg, R. G., M. R. Liebowitz, D. A. Hope, and F. R. Schneier, eds. 1995. *Social Phobia: Diagnosis, Assessment, and Treatment.* New York: Guilford Press.

Hofmann, S. G., and P. M. DiBartolo. 2001. *From Social Anxiety to Social Phobia: Multiple Perspectives.* Needham Heights, MA: Allyn and Bacon.

Rapee, R. M., and W. C. Sanderson. 1998. *Social Phobia: Clinical Application of Evidence-Based Psychotherapy.* Northvale, NJ: Jason Aronson.

Schmidt, L. A., and J. Schulkin, eds. 1999. *Extreme Fear, Shyness and Social Phobia: Origins, Biological Mechanisms, and Clinical Outcomes.* New York: Oxford University Press.

Stein, M. B., ed. 1995. *Social Phobia: Clinical and Research Perspectives.* Washington, DC: American Psychiatric Press.

Turk, C., R. G. Heimberg, and D. A. Hope. 2001. Social anxiety disorder. In *Clinical Handbook of Psychological Disorders, 3rd* ed., edited by D. H. Barlow. New York: Guilford Press.

Video Resources

Rapee, R. M. 1999. *I Think They Think . . . Overcoming Social Phobia* (videotape). New York: Guilford Publications.

References

Antony, M. M., and R. E. McCabe. 2003. Anxiety disorders: Social and specific phobias. In *Psychiatry*, 2nd ed., edited by A. Tasman, J. Kay, and J. A. Lieberman. Chichester, UK: John Wiley and Sons.

Antony, M. M., C. L. Purdon, V. Huta, and R. P. Swinson. 1998. Dimensions of perfectionism across the anxiety disorders. *Behaviour Research and Therapy* 36:1143-1154.

Antony, M. M., K. Rowa, A. Liss, S. Swallow, and R. P. Swinson. In press. Social comparison processes in social phobia. *Behavior Therapy*.

Antony, M. M., and R. P. Swinson. 1998. *When Perfect Isn't Good Enough: Strategies for Coping with Perfectionism*. Oakland, CA: New Harbinger Publications.

Antony, M. M., and R. P. Swinson. 2000. *The Shyness and Social Anxiety Workbook: Proven, Step-by-Step Techniques for Overcoming Your Fear*. Oakland, CA: New Harbinger Publications.

Beck, A. T., and G. Emery (with R. Greenberg). 1985. *Anxiety Disorders and Phobias: A Cognitive Perspective*. New York: Basic Books.

Bolton, R. 1979. *People Skills*. New York: Simon & Schuster.

Bowman, D. P. 1998. *Presentations: Proven Techniques for Creating Presentations That Get Results*. Holbrook, MA: Adams Media Corporation.

Browne, J. 1997. *Dating for Dummies*. Foster City, CA: IDG Books Worldwide.

Buchan, V. 1997. *Make Presentations with Confidence,* 2nd ed. Hauppauge, NY: Barron's Educational Series.

Burns, D. D. 1999. *The Feeling Good Handbook*. Revised edition. New York: Plume.

Carducci, B. J., and P. G. Zimbardo. 1995. Are you shy? *Psychology Today* November/December, pp. 34-40, 64, 66, 68, 70, 78, 82.

Cornwall, B., and D. C. Lundgren. 2001. Love on the Internet: Involvement and misrepresentation in romantic relationships in cyberspace vs. realspace. *Computers in Human Behavior* 17:197-211.

Davidson, J. 2003. *The Complete Guide to Public Speaking*. Hoboken, NJ: Wiley.

Dils, T. E. 2003. *Mother Teresa: Humanitarian and Religious Leader*. Broomall, PA: Chelsea House Publishers.

Dorio, M. 2000. *The Complete Idiot's Guide to the Perfect Interview,* 2nd ed. Indianapolis, IN: Alpha Books.

Fleming, J. 1997. *Become Assertive!* Kent, UK: David Grant Publishing.

Foa, E. B., M. E. Franklin, K. J. Perry, and J. D. Herbert. 1996. Cognitive biases in generalized social phobia. *Journal of Abnormal Psychology* 105:433-439.

Furmark, T., M. Tillfors, I. Marteinsdottir, H. Fischer, A. Pissiota, et al. 2002. Common changes in cerebral blood flow in patients with social phobia treated with citalopram or cognitive-behavioral therapy. *Archives of General Psychiatry* 59:425-433.

Garner, A. 1997. *Conversationally Speaking: Testing New Ways to Increase Your Personal and Social Effectiveness,* 3rd ed. Los Angeles: Lowell House.

Gould, R. A., and G. A. Clum. 1995. Self-help plus minimal therapist contact in the treatment of panic disorder: A replication and extension. *Behavior Therapy* 26:533-546.

Hecker, J. E., M. C. Losee, B. K. Fritzler, and C. M. Fink. 1996. Self-directed versus therapist-directed cognitive behavioral treatment for panic disorder. *Journal of Anxiety Disorders* 10:253-265.

Heimberg, R. G., and R. E. Becker. 2002. *Cognitive-Behavioral Group Therapy for Social Phobia: Basic Mechanisms and Clinical Strategies.* New York: Guilford.

Henderson, L., and P. G. Zimbardo. 1999. Shyness. In *Encyclopedia of Mental Health*, edited by H. S. Friedman. San Diego, CA: Academic Press.

Hofmann, S. G., and D. H. Barlow. 2002. Social phobia (social anxiety disorder). In *Anxiety and Its Disorders: The Nature and Treatment of Anxiety and Panic*, 2nd ed., edited by D. H. Barlow. New York: Guilford Publications.

Holle, C., J. H. Neely, and R. G. Heimberg. 1997. The effects of blocked versus random presentation and semantic relatedness of stimulus words on response to a modified Stroop task among social phobics. *Cognitive Therapy and Research* 21:681-697.

Honeychurch, C., and A. Watrous. 2003. *Talk to Me: Conversation Tips for the Small-Talk Challenged.* Oakland, CA: New Harbinger Publications.

Kennedy, J. L. 2000. *Job Interviews for Dummies*, 2nd ed. New York: Hungry Minds.

Knox, D., V. Daniels, L. Sturdivant, and M. E. Zusman. 2001. College student use of the Internet for mate selection. *College Student Journal* 35:158-160.

Kuriansky, J. 1999. *The Complete Idiot's Guide to Dating*, 2nd ed. New York: Alpha Books.

Kushner, M. 1996. *Successful Presentations for Dummies.* Foster City, CA: IDG Books Worldwide.

Laumann, E. O., J. H. Gagnon, R. T. Michael, and S. Michaels. 1994. *The Social Organization of Sexuality: Sexual Practices in the United States.* Chicago, IL: University of Chicago Press.

Lundh, L.-G., and L.-G. Öst, 1996. Recognition bias for critical faces in social phobics. *Behaviour Research and Therapy* 34:787-794.

McCabe, R. E., M. M. Antony, L. J. Summerfeldt, A. Liss, and R. P. Swinson. 1993. A preliminary examination of the relationship between anxiety disorders in adults and self-reported history of teasing or bullying experiences. *Cognitive Behaviour Therapy* 4:187-193.

McCown, J. A., D. Fischer, R. Page, and M. Homant. 2001. Internet relationships: People who meet other people. *Cyberpsychology and Behavior* 4:593-596.

McKay, M., M. Davis, and P. Fanning. 1995. *Messages: The Communications Skills Book,* 2nd ed. Oakland, CA: New Harbinger Publications.

Morgan, H., and C. Raffle. 1999. Does reducing safety behaviours improve treatment response in patients with social phobia? *Australia and New Zealand Journal of Psychiatry* 33:503-510.

Mulkens, S., P. J. de Jong, A. Dobbelaar, and S. M. Bögels. 1999. Fear of blushing: Fearful preoccupation irrespective of facial coloration. *Behaviour Research and Therapy* 37: 1119-1128.

Nice, M. L., and R. Katzev. 1998. Internet romances: The frequency and nature of on-line relationships. *Cyberpsychology and Behavior* 1:217-223.

Norton, P. J., and D. A. Hope. 2001. Kernels of truth or distorted perceptions: Self and observer ratings of social anxiety and performance. *Behavior Therapy* 32:765-786.

Nurnberg, H. G., P. L. Hensley, A. J. Gelenberg, M. Fava, J. Lauriello, and S. Paine. 2003. Treatment of antidepressant-associated sexual dysfunction with sildenafil: A randomized controlled trial. *Journal of the American Medical Association* 289:56-64.

Paterson, R. J. 2000. *The Assertiveness Workbook: How to Express Your Ideas and Stand Up for Yourself at Work and in Relationships.* Oakland, CA: New Harbinger Publications.

Purdon, C., M. M. Antony, S. Monteiro, and R. P. Swinson. 2001. Social anxiety in college students. *Journal of Anxiety Disorders* 15:203-215.

Rapee, R. M., and L. Lim. 1992. Discrepancy between self- and observer ratings of performance in social phobics. *Journal of Abnormal Psychology* 101:728-731.

Rapee, R. M., and W. C. Sanderson. 1998. *Social Phobia: Clinical Application of Evidence-Based Psychotherapy.* Northvale, NJ: Jason Aronson.

Roth, D., M. M. Antony, and R. P. Swinson. 2001. Interpretations for anxiety symptoms in social phobia. *Behaviour Research and Therapy* 39:129-138.

Roy-Byrne, P. P., and D. S. Cowley. 2002. Pharmacological treatments for panic disorder, generalized anxiety disorder, specific phobia, and social anxiety disorder. In *A Guide to Treatments That Work,* 2nd ed., edited by P. E. Nathan and J. M. Gorman. New York: Oxford University Press.

Sebba, A. 1998. *Mother Teresa: Beyond the Image.* New York: Doubleday.

Stein, M. 2003. *Fearless Interviewing: How to Win the Job by Communicating with Confidence.* New York: McGraw-Hill.

Stein, M. B., M. J. Chartier, A. L. Hazen, M. V. Kozak, M. E. Tancer, S. Lander, et al. 1998. A direct-interview family study of generalized social phobia. *American Journal of Psychiatry* 155:90-97.

Stein, M. B., J. R. Walker, and D. R. Forde. 1994. Setting diagnostic thresholds for social phobia: Considerations from a community survey of social anxiety. *American Journal of Psychiatry* 151:408-412.

Stopa, L., and D. M. Clark. 1993. Cognitive processes in social phobia. *Behaviour Research and Therapy* 31:255-267.

Tessina, T. 1998. *The Unofficial Guide to Dating Again.* New York: Macmillan.

Tillfors, M., T. Furmark, I. Marteinsdottir, H. Fischer, A. Pissiota, B. Langstrom, et al. 2001. Cerebral blood flow in subjects with social phobia during stressful speaking tasks: A PET study. *American Journal of Psychiatry* 158:1220-1226.

Tillfors, M., T. Furmark, I. Marteinsdottir, and M. Fredrikson. 2002. Cerebral blood flow during anticipation of public speaking in social phobia: A PET study. *Biological Psychiatry* 52:1113-1119.

Wells, A., D. M. Clark, P. Salkovskis, J. Ludgate, A. Hackman, and M. Gelder. 1995. Social phobia: The role of in-situation safety behaviors in maintaining anxiety and negative beliefs. *Behavior Therapy* 26:153-161.

Winton, E. C., D. M. Clark, and R. J. Edelmann. 1995. Social anxiety, fear of negative evaluation and the detection of negative emotion in others. *Behaviour Research and Therapy* 33:193-196.

Zimbardo, P. G., P. A. Pilkonis, and R. M. Norwood. 1975. The social disease of shyness. *Psychology Today* 8:68-72.

About the Author

MARTIN M. ANTONY, PH.D., is a Professor in the Department of Psychiatry and Behavioural Neurosciences at McMaster University. He is also the Chief Psychologist and Director of the Anxiety Treatment and Research Centre at St. Joseph's Healthcare in Hamilton, Ontario. He has published eleven books and more than eighty articles and book chapters in the areas of cognitive behavioral therapy, panic disorder, social phobia, specific phobia, and obsessive-compulsive disorder. Dr. Antony has received early career awards from the Society of Clinical Psychology (American Psychological Association), the Canadian Psychological Association, and the Anxiety Disorders Association of America, and is a Fellow of the American and Canadian Psychological Associations. He was recently President of the Anxiety Disorders Special Interest Group of the Association for Advancement of Behavior Therapy (AABT) and was Program Chair for the 2001 AABT meeting, as well as for the 2003 convention of the Anxiety Disorders Association of America. Dr. Antony is actively involved in clinical research in the area of anxiety disorders, teaching and education, and maintains a clinical practice.

Some Other New Harbinger Titles

The Daily Relaxer, Item 4542 $14.95

What's Right With Me, Item 4429 $16.95

10 Simple Solutions to Migraines, Item 4410 $12.95

10 Simple Solutions to Adult ADD, Item 4348 $12.95

How to Stop Backing Down & Start Talking Back, Item 4178 $13.95

The Self-Esteem Guided Journal, Item 402X $13.95

Five Good Minutes, Item 4143 $12.95

The Emotional House, Item 4089 $14.95

Talk to Me, Item 3317 $12.95

Romantic Intelligence, Item 3309 $15.95

Eating Mindfully, Item 3503 $13.95

Sex Talk, Item 2868 $12.95

Everyday Adventures for the Soul, Item 2981 $11.95

The Daughter-In-Law's Survival Guide, Item 2817 $12.95

Love Tune-Ups, Item 2744 $10.95

Brave New You, Item 2590 $13.95

The Conscious Bride, Item 2132 $12.95

Juicy Tomatoes, Item 2175 $14.95

Fifty Great Tips, Tricks, and Techniques to Connect with Your Teen, Item 3597 $10.95

The Well-Ordered Home, Item 321X $12.95

Call **toll free, 1-800-748-6273,** or log on to our online bookstore at **www.newharbinger.com** to order. Have your Visa or Mastercard number ready. Or send a check for the titles you want to New Harbinger Publications, Inc., 5674 Shattuck Ave., Oakland, CA 94609. Include $4.50 for the first book and 75¢ for each additional book, to cover shipping and handling. (California residents please include appropriate sales tax.) Allow two to five weeks for delivery.

Prices subject to change without notice.